RCI:
The Secret
Organization

Samuel D. Webster

CLF Publishing, LLC.

9161 Sierra Ave, Ste. 203C
Fontana, CA 92335
www.clfpublishing.org

Cover Design by Senir Design. Contact information- info@senirdesign.com.

ISBN # 978-1-945102-07-3

Printed in the United States of America.

Dedications

This book is dedicated to my mother,
Catherine Webster
and to my sister,
Antoinette Anderson

Acknowledgements

I acknowledge my long-time friends,
Renée, Yvonne, and Dr. Peterson
for their years of support.
Also, I acknowledge my publisher and editor,
Dr. Cassundra White-Elliott
for all her help on this project.

Dedications

This book is dedicated to my mother,
Catherine Webster
and to my sister,
Antoinette Anderson

Acknowledgements

I acknowledge my long-time friends,
Renée, Yvonne, and Dr. Peterson
for their years of support.
Also, I acknowledge my publisher and editor,
Dr. Cassundra White-Elliott
for all her help on this project.

The Premature Ending...

At 8:00 a.m. my alarm went off. I jumped up, and I yelled out, "Shit!" I had set my clock incorrectly. I rushed as fast as I could to take a shower. I had that feeling that we all get once in a while that that day was not going to be a good day. That was not my first time being late on the job, but I was thinking to myself that it might be my last time. When I got there, I punched in and walked quickly down the hall trying not to be noticed. Then out of the middle of nowhere, there he was: Willie, the boss. I almost froze and became nervous as hell.

He said, "Hi. How are you doing today, Samuel?"

I said, "Fine, and how about yourself, sir?"

He said, "Great." Then, he said, "This is your last damn time being late. One more time and you are out of here! Do I make myself clear?"

I said, "Yes, sir." When he walked away, I took a deep breath and said, "Thank you, God."

When I went in and started work, I looked and saw how no one was saying a word, as if they were mute. I had been with the company going on three years and had never seen anyone like that before, especially the people I had met when I first started there. As lunchtime drew near, Tina tapped me on my shoulder and said, "Let's eat here at the cafeteria. I will explain why it was so quiet when you got here this evening." Tina was a great person and one of the first people I met when I started at RCI. Of all the ladies there, she was the main one I had strong feelings for. As she and I went into the cafeteria, it looked as if all the workers were there that day. I looked and saw people that I knew well. David, James, and Rita had worked for the company for a long time. These people all had different personalities. David was the type of person who could tell a lie in a minute and have a straight look on his face, so much that he could get you to believe him. James was the kind who would do a favor for you and would never ask for anything in return for it. Rita had one of the nicest smiles you had ever seen.

As they sat not too far from us, they tried to hear the conversation Tina and I were having. Tina put her arms around me and said in my ear, "There is an investigation into the company." When she said that, my eyes stood up. I began to have flashbacks to when I first start working for RCI in December of 1999.

Something happened one day on the job that I will never forget. It was a payday. That day and that week was one of the highest pay weeks for me since working for the company. Tina, Nancy, and Michael asked me if I wanted to go to the liquor store or wait until the next day to cash my check. As we continued to talk, I looked and behold, there were four white men in suits. They were clean shaven, with short hair and shade glasses. The suits they wore were not the average ones that a man could afford to buy. Something told me these guys were not the regular guys you see in the store everyday or talk with on the street.

As soon as they went into the office in the back, Matthew went in also. He was the boss at that time at RCI. He was about 6'2" tall, a white man who was like a cowboy and was originally from Texas. While I was at RCI, he treated everyone with respect, but he didn't take any shit off anyone. Believe it or not, when Matthew came out the office, all of us looked at him for an answer as if to say, "What is going on." While we stood there, the four white men in suits came out and said to Matthew, "Thanks for your cooperation." Then, they left.

All of us, who were mostly African Americans, except for Hosea, who was Latino, but we still considered him as our brother, stood there looking, wondering what was going on.

Matthew called all of us to the side of the building and said, "Look, I don't want any of you to panic about what I'm about to tell you. Those guys that y'all saw, this is not their first time here. Some of you were here when they came a year and half ago." Then, he said something that agitated all of us. "They are with the FBI." Then, it crossed my mind that there were four men in suits there before but with different faces. Matthew was in charge, but he was not one of the big guys running the company who made the decisions. What surprised me about RCI when I first started working there was the acquisitions and expenditures that were going on. I was surprised because the company was a family business with husbands, wives, sons, daughters, nephews, nieces, and cousins that work there.

On the evening shift, Matthew told all us to go back to work. He said we had nothing to worry about; plus, they had nothing on us. However, the others and I knew there had to be a reason why the FBI came back, and Matthew knew something but didn't say anything. We found out later, he made a deal with them in the office. We were thinking he was really our friend.

Then on May 15, 2003, something happened that would change all of us for the rest of our lives. Something we would never forget. The same way no one in America will ever forget where he/she was during the 9/11 tragedy.

About 6:00 p.m. the Prince George County Police and the postal inspectors came running in and shouted, "PUT YOUR HANDS UP NOW, ALL OF YOU, AND DON'T MOVE!" I heard someone in the back say, "Oh shit! They got us now!"

That day, RCI the secret organization came to an end. Eight people were arrested for money laundering and racketeering.

The Phenomenon of Heartbreak

My story begins in the year 1998, when I lived at 5805 N. Longfellow St. Apt. 2, in Arlington, VA. During that time, I worked at Macy's in Pentagon City. No, it was not the best job in the world, but as the saying goes- it was a job. Having been there almost a year, it seemed like nothing was really changing. The company was hiring for the Christmas season, so other workers and I went to the back of the office to meet the new workers and give them instructions. When I first lay my eyes on one of the new workers, I couldn't take them off. Her name was Paula. Mr. Robinson, the manager of Macy's, told me to show her around. I said, "It would be my honor, sir." Other new workers were being shown around by other senior workers.

I smiled, introduced myself and said, "Welcome to the company of Macy's," and shook her hand. As we walked around the store, she told me a little about herself, such as how she was transferring to Macy's in Arlington, VA but lived in the Adams Morgan area. When she said that, my eyes went up. Before I could respond, she told me she had another job making far more money, but I didn't get in her business, by asking her, "Oh, Paula, how much?" Paula was from St. Louis, and she wanted to get away from that city for some time.

She asked me, "Where are you from? You have a deep southern accent."

I replied, "From Washington, DC. But after some time, my family moved to Manassas, VA when my father got a job at the Pentagon."

She asked, "Is your father still working at the Pentagon?"

I replied, "My father passed away years ago, but my mother is living in Dale City, VA, where my sister lives."

Paula inquired, "Do you have a girlfriend?"

"I did, but she and I broke up some time ago." I asked her, "Are you seeing anyone?"

She said, "Not at this time, but I will be soon. I'm looking at him now."

When she said that, I started smiling thinking to myself, *God may have sent this beautiful, intelligent lady to me, and it couldn't have happened at a better time.* Then, I asked Paula if she would like to go out the next day for lunch, saying the treat was on me.

She replied, "Most certainly." When she said that, I was a little shocked because I thought she was going to say no. When I was finished showing her around the store, we went back to the office where the other workers were. We were about ten minutes late. Mr. Robinson didn't say anything. However, he had a look on his face, as if to say, *Samuel, you have a deep crush on that girl. I can see it on you.*

When I got home, my phone started ringing. It was my sister. I had that feeling when I picked up the phone that she was going to ask me about my day and if I had met someone.

"What are you doing?" she asked.

"I just got off work about 30 minutes ago."

She asked, "How was it at work?"

"Today, it was pretty good."

"You sound like you hit the number!"

I laughed; then, I said, "Why do you say that?"

"Something happened today."

Afterward, I said in my mind, *Oh, what the hell? I'll tell her.* I told her I met an attractive lady on the job.

"Okay, but I hope you know what you're doing," she said.

I replied, "I do." My sister always gave me advice. She was like a second mother. Even before I started kindergarten, she would always bring me a cookie home when she got out of class.

When I got off the phone with her, I said to myself, *Why does she have to think like that? What if it were her? She can't be more positive instead of negative?* Then, I remembered what my mom and dad once said about my sister: She acts the way she does because she cares for you.

When morning came, I stopped at Roy Rodgers for breakfast at the Ballston Mall, which is in Arlington. After eating, I started thinking deeply about whether something good or bad was going to happen. I would always meditate for a few minutes. I have always tried to be a positive thinker although I did not have all the facts. Confucius once said, "We have become what our thoughts have made us."

As I left the mall to catch the bus that went into DC, I heard a voice that said, "Samuel." I turned and looked, and there was Paula in a BMW asking me, "You need a ride, Mr. Webster?" with that beautiful smile on her face.

I responded, "Well, I don't know. My parents always taught me to never get in a car with strangers." When I said that, we both started to laugh, as I got into the car. It took twenty minutes before we got to work.

When we went in, Paula said, "I would like to show you the area I work in on the fourth floor."

I responded, "I would be honored." I reminded her about lunch, and she showed interest. I asked her if Sizzlers would be okay.

"That would be fine," she replied.

Time passed. From the time Paula had started working at Macys, my sales had doubled. But was it because of her? Or, was it a coincidence or because Christmas was near. It could have been either.

My feelings for that special lady continued to grow, but I tried not to show it. However, she could tell. As we went to lunch one day, we talked while holding one another's hands and kissing. After that, I said in my mind, *Without a shadow of a doubt, God sent this beautiful woman to me to be in my life.* While thinking deeply on that, Paula took my hand and put it on her face and said, "You are day dreaming." After saying that, she said, "I have to watch you."

I said, "You must be able to read my mind. You truly knew I was thinking about you."

At the end of the day, when work was over, I said to her, "I would like to show you where I live sometime." She asked if it was in walking distance.

"It's not too far when walking but getting on the bus would get you there in about ten minutes."

She said, "I would like to see where you live."

When she said that, I said, "Let's go." When we got there, I said, "Here it is: Westover Apartments."

She looked and said, "These apartments are very nice."

I told her, "I live a little ways up the hill in Apartment 2."

As we went in, she saw the living room, which was in the front as you come in. Then, the kitchen was in the back. The upstairs on the left side was the bedroom. Inside, those apartments actually looked like houses. As we both sat down, I wanted to tell her how much I loved her and wanted to be with her, but I became inarticulate. I got up and went to the kitchen and got some snacks. Then, I turned on the TV, and there it was one of my favorite shows: "Good Times," showing John Amos putting his arms around Esther Rolle, telling her just how much he loved her.

After hearing those words, I couldn't hold back any longer. I put my arms around her and deeply kissed her, telling her how much I loved and cared for her and had the expectation that we would get married one day.

After watching TV, we went upstairs and lay in bed together in love. I was the Romeo, and she was the Juliet, but we wanted to live not die. I had that affection for her that I had never had for any other woman, and she saw that.

When I woke up the next morning, she was gone. I called her name, as I was thinking she was in the bathroom. But, she wasn't. I went down the stairs, and I saw how the living room and kitchen were clean and put in place.

I looked and saw by the side of the lamp a note from Paula that said, "I'm very sorry, Samuel, but I can't do this. Please forgive me." I became almost sick to my stomach, not knowing what to think. I left my apartment in a hurry to catch the bus as quickly as possible. When I got to work, I went immediately up to the fourth floor were Paula worked. Her supervisor told me she quit. When I heard those words, I felt like my world was falling apart. I went downstairs as fast as I could. When I got there, Mr. Robinson was showing some workers from another Macy's around. When I saw him, he called me, but I didn't answer.

When I left out, I got on the subway across the street and went to Washington, DC. I went to the Adams Morgan Apartments where Paula lived. As I went in, the security guard asked me, "Can I help you?" I told him I was looking for Paula Smith and that she had not shown up for work that day. He told me she had moved from the apartments that morning. Then, he said, "She had two people help her put her things in a U-Haul." I asked the guard about her car, and he said she sold it to some foreigners who did not live there in the building.

I left feeling like my whole world had come to an end, but things would only get worse. When I got back to work, one of the salesmen who I had never seen before asked me, "Are you Samuel?"

I looked at him in a strange way and said, "Yes, I am."

He said, "Mr. Robinson wants to see you in his office."

I immediately said to myself, "Oh, brother."

When I walked into his office, I felt a little agitation. Mr. Robinson said to me, "Mr. Webster…" That was the first time he had ever called me by my last name. While smoking a cigar, he said, "You really embarrassed me right in front of my employees visiting here from other states. I'm going to tell you right in your face: Get your last check and go! You are fired!"

When I got my check from the office, Pam, one of the workers who worked with Paula, was also picking up her check. She knew the whole story and what had happened. She looked at me and said, "I feel for you. You really love her."

I said, "Yes." When I got home, I sat down, just looking at the walls in the living room for three nights. I lay on the floor in the living room, looking up and asking myself, "Is this how it was supposed to end? What am I going to do now?"

As I looked up, I thought of a song I used to hear my relatives play, "Everybody Plays a Fool Sometimes." When I got back up, I sat in the chair again. I noticed something on the walls in the living room. As I ogled it, I realized I had not seen it before, and it petrified the hell out of me. It looked just like the walls were sweating or if tears were coming down. My heart started jumping at a fast beat. I felt as if I were having a heart attack. I began to feel as if I couldn't move.

After taking an immensely deep breath, I was finally able to move myself and go over to the wall. I felt it, but nothing was there. It was not wet at all. Was my mind playing tricks on me? That was something I couldn't grasp. I started to go up the stairs to my bedroom; then, I caught myself and said, "I can't do this."

I then turned back and headed to the kitchen. When I got there, I saw something outside the window that surprised me but was filled with ecstasy: Two squirrels were kissing one another. I had seen those small animals many times, but that was the first time I had ever seen them kiss one another. I started thinking what if Paula and I were those two squirrels, would we still be together?

Then, things started running through my mind, such as *Is reincarnation real? Do people come back as other people or animals?* There have been many stories told and written on the subject. Whether it's a fact or myth, it gives people something to think about. How would I feel if I came back to the earth as a different person or animal? That's a question I don't think anyone could answer.

As I sat at the table in the kitchen eating cereal and meditating on how to overcome the relationship, I tried to put my mind and father's mind together to see what my father's thoughts would be. When growing up in the city of Washington, DC, my father was my best friend, and he is the reason I don't have a criminal record.

As I sat in the kitchen with my eyes closed and holding my breath, the first thought I had was, *You have to move on with your life. There are always more fish in the sea.* As the words continued to go around in my mind, for a moment, it felt like it was working. Then, I burst out yelling!

I made a promise never to sleep in that bedroom again, where the lady I thought loved me slept with me. After the third day, I finally accepted reality- that I needed help. I had been in it for three days locked away from the world, but it felt like thirty days when I went out.

Mrs. Johnson yelled at me, "How are you, Samuel?" She was originally from Ireland and watched everyone in the neighborhood. You could have lost everything you had. If anything happened in the neighborhood, Mrs. Johnson would know about it.

"Where is that sweetheart of yours?" I believe she saw Paula when she was leaving because no one had seen her when we had arrived to my apartment. Also, I believe Mrs. Johnson could detect that I was upset when she saw me. I was taught not to lie by my parents, but that time I had to tell one.

"She went on vacation," I said.

She responded, "When she gets back, bring her over. I would like to meet her."

I said, "Okay, Mrs. Johnson," knowing that it would never happen.

Arriving at DC General Hospital, as I went in, Renée was right there. She was one of my doctor's nurses, who later would become a doctor herself. She was the one that I had a close relationship with that could have led to marriage. She was the girl whom my mother wanted me to marry.

As I started to talk with Renée, I was smiling, trying as hard as I could not to show that something had happened, but as we men know, somehow women can tell when something has happened- good or bad. As we were talking, Renée looked at me right in the face and said, "What is wrong, Samuel?"

I respond, "Nothing."

Then, she said, "You know I can see through you. Okay, but you will tell me later." I hated when she said that because she was right. She picked up the phone and called Dr. Peterson's office to tell him I was there, and that I wanted to see him. Dr. Peterson was our family doctor and had graduated from Howard University back in the 80's. My father knew him back during that time.

When I went in, he asked me, "What is wrong? You look troubled." I told him the whole story of what happened, how I slept on the floor for three days and nights, and what I felt like doing. He said unto me, "What are you trying to tell me, Samuel?"

I told him I thought about committing suicide although it had never crossed my mind before. I believe it crosses everyone's mind at least once in their lifetime; it even crossed Moses' mind.

"Dr. Peterson," I said, "I feel like killing myself and there is nothing left for me in this world. Why should I live in it?"

He looked at me and said with a serious tone, "You do something like that, and you will surely go right to hell. You think you are suffering now. You ain't felt nothing yet. When a person goes there, there is no turning back."

When I walked out his office, Renée asked me, "How did it go?"

I responded, "It was okay. I feel a little better." But, Renée knew I was concealing something. In time, I would tell her what happened. After I hugged her, I left. She told me to keep in contact with her. When I got back to Arlington, VA, I still felt an absence in me. A person could have shot me with a gun, and I swear I would have never felt it. When I got to Ballston Station, I decided to go to the mall to the food court. As I went in, I saw how filled it was with people.

I had been to that mall off and on, but that was the first time I had been to its food court. It was almost 12:00. After I ordered something from Hardes, I walked around looking for somewhere to sit and eat. It looked as though it was impossible at first until I found a spot all the way in the back. As I sat and ate, I looked and saw how there were couples together eating and enjoying themselves. The looks they had on their faces showed how much they cared for each other. I thought, *That's how I feel about Paula.*

After eating, I was in a deep daze until someone tapped me on the shoulder. I looked, and it was Stephen, one of the guys I grew up with; we went to the same high school. He asked how my mom and sister were doing.

I said, "Fine. They are living in Dale City, VA.

He asked, "How is your father?"

"He passed away years ago."

"I'm sorry," he said. "How about Renée? Did y'all ever get married?"

I was silent for a while. Then, I said, "No."

"Where are you working at, man?"

"I just got fired."

"That's too bad," he responded. I looked and noticed some guys were coming to the table, but before they got there they yelled, "Stephen, it's time to go."

He said, "Samuel, the company I work for Resource Consultants, Inc., in Capitol Heights, MD is hiring." When he said that, I looked and noticed the strange uniforms he and the other employees were wearing, but I didn't say anything. I asked what kind of company it was.

He said, "RCI, as it is called, has a contract with the post office. Samuel, I remember when your father worked for a company in Upper Marlboro, MD called Mail Express." I was very surprised he remembered the company my father worked for. He then said, "The work is similar to Mail Express work."

The guys that were with him interrupted saying, "Stephen, come on. We are waiting."

He shook my hand and said, "Think on it."

I said, "I will. Peace."

As soon as I got back home, there it was- something I didn't want to see: a note from my landlord stating how I owed half of the rent from last month. As I went inside my apartment, I became very depressed, like I was getting ready to have a nervous breakdown. I fell down and lay on the floor for hours. To me, life didn't mean anything anymore.

Getting My Life on Track

I said, "God, my name, my date of birth, my records here on earth, let all of this be gone. I never was born, nor did I ever exist. People that know me let them no more remember me. Let another man replace me and become my mother's son. Lord, let me find a home in the world of purgatory." After I said those words, I lifted my head and saw something that I couldn't identify. Even to this very day, all I can say about it is it was some kind of life form sitting in the corner of the living room looking straight at me. It said, "You lost the woman that you love plus your job, and now you are about to lose your apartment. What are you going do now, Mr. Big Shot?"

I look to the right side where the stairs were located and started to walk up them, but then I caught myself. I had said I would never go to that bedroom again. As I went back down, the voice from the life form, that could make anyone have a massive heart attack, said unto me, "You have to sleep somewhere tonight." When the life form said that, it stood there rubbing its hands together. I looked to the right side of the living room where the closet was just before the kitchen and decided to sleep there for the night. I remembered the time I entered the closet. It was 9:15 pm. There was a clock above the refrigerator, and I looked at it before closing the door. I left the kitchen light on that night.

The night seemed like it went by fast as I lay my head down and closed my eyes just for a minute. Before I knew it, it was day. I saw a little light at the bottom of the door as I got up and went out. The sun was shining, and I looked to the corner of the living room and the spirit of life form was no longer there. For some odd reason, I started thinking of the classic novel *The Devil and Daniel Webster*. To this day, I still ask myself was it real or a dream or was I just having a hallucination.

As I prepared for the day, I washed my hands and face in the kitchen, still not wanting to go up those stairs. Then, I left out, hoping not to run into Mrs. Johnson, my nosey next-door neighbor. As I got on the bus, I continued saying to myself, "What are you going to do? You've got to do something, but what?"

When I arrived to Ballston Station, I stood there for a couple of minutes. Then, it crossed my mind about the company RCI that one of my friends told me about and how they were hiring. Talking to myself in my mind, I said, *Even if I get a job with them right away, I would still have to find a place in Prince George County, MD to live.* "How can I do this?" I asked myself. "As of right now, I have nothing." I decided to take a chance and go to Maryland to at least try to find something.

When I got there, there were so many apartments. It was almost impossible to check them all in one day. They all were different, and the rent was just unbelievable for the ones I went to. That went on for days: going to Maryland then going back home, ducking Mrs. Johnson when I left out in the morning. But that was the least thing to worry about. My time was running out. Also, I was short on money from catching the bus and the subway to Maryland.

Finally, I stopped and said to myself, "I have to start looking in the Washington Post for apartments to lease. That will save me time and money." As I looked through the paper day after day, I found nothing. I was starting to have that feeling of absence, which we all have once in a while. I was almost ready to give up, until I said, "God, I brought these things upon myself. Please give me a chance to get back on my feet."

As I looked back in the paper again, there it was: an apartment for $449 a month. I could be wrong, but I had not seen that article in the paper before asking God for help. As my parents always said to me and my sister, "God works in mysterious ways." I thought to myself, *An apartment for that price can't be all that great.* But in my right mind, I had to take what I could find at that time with all the things that were going on. The apartments that I saw in the Washington Post, that were renting for a low price, didn't have a name, just a number. I called and spoke with the landlord. She sounded like a very nice person who could work something out.

I asked her if the next day would be okay go in to fill out an application. She said that would be fine. She sound very alluring on the phone, or should I say charming. I asked the name of the apartments, and she replied, "Hillside Heights." When she responded, it rang a bell. I started thinking to myself, *I have heard of those apartments.* While in deep thought, I heard somebody say, "Hello, are you still there?

I said, "Yes." After that, I asked which street the apartments were located on.

She said, "123 Marlboro Pike. Take the 16 or the 14, and it will bring you right here."

I asked, "What would be the best time to come?"

"1:00 pm," she said.

Then, I replied, "That will be fine. If you don't mind what is your name?"

"Antoinette."

"That is my sister's name."

She laughed then said, "I will see you tomorrow, Samuel."

"Okay."

When I got off the phone, I was trying to remember those apartments and where I heard of them before. Then, I put that to the side and start thinking of my chances of getting a place there with the month being almost over. *If I move there, the first thing I'm going do is contact Stephen about getting hired at RCI,* I thought.

The next day, I went to the apartments at Hillside Heights, as they were called. The front part of the complex looked very nice. As I went to the rental office, there she was sitting at the desk talking on the phone. She looked at me, smiled and said, "I will be with you in a minute." I noticed the smile she had on her face and how she spoke on the phone. She had eyeglasses on that made her look very attractive. After about five minutes on the phone, she got up and walked around, shook my hand, and said, "Samuel, welcome to Hillside Heights Apartments."

I responded, "Thank you." She turned back, sat down at the desk, pulled out an application, and gave it to me.

"Fill this out as best as you can. If you need any help, let me know immediately." The way she said that and the leniency she had was awesome. My feelings for her started to grow until I caught myself saying, *Look, you have not gotten over Paula. Heal yourself first before going into another relationship.* When I was almost finished with the application, there were some questions that were tricky to answer. That's when I asked for her assistance.

She responded, "Yes, I will," with that nice smile and explained to me what I didn't understand. She did it in a professional manner. When the application was finished, I glanced through it and signed my signature. Most people give their signature before reading the fine print. And that's what I did, but then there was a problem: the deposit.

I had the first month's rent $449 plus a $100 deposit, but I had never asked her how much the deposit was. You see, I was saving money to move eventually because I really wanted to leave Macy's, find a better job, and move to another location. That was the time to see how kind she really was. I took a deep breath and said, "I have $100 for the deposit."

She looked and said, "That's okay, but the deposit is $150, but we will work this out." She showed her kindness right then.

I said, "Antoinette, I didn't tell you over the phone."

She replied, "About not having all the deposit?"

I said, "No, that's not it."

"What is it?"

I said, "That my sister's name is Antoinette also."

She said, "Samuel, be honest with me."

I said, "That's the God's honest truth."

She said, "Okay, I'm going show you your apartment now. You will be in apartment 105." I asked her if the apartment I was going be in would look like the front apartments. When I said that, she had a strange look on her face and that made me very cautious. When we left out the building, we turned right and went down the back. As we came to the second building, it looked good but not like the first.

Then, the third was a substitution as well. I had a feeling that the fourth building was going to be really different. When we got there and I saw it, I was completed devastated by what I saw. Then, I looked at Antoinette, and before I could open my mouth and say anything, she said, "Let me explain. First, I would like to apologize. The article in the paper did not explain or reveal that some of the apartments are different than others in this complex or that the architecture of all the buildings is not the same. I would like to apologize. Here in Prince George County, as you may know, the rent is very high. Other than this apartment, the lowest one you are going to find is one for $650 a month and that doesn't include the utilities." After saying that, she said, "Do you still want the place?"

I stood speechless thinking to myself, *This place didn't turn out the way I thought it would, but then like she said, 'Where would I find a place cheaper than this?'* I was also thinking about how I probably was going be evicted back at my apartment in Arlington, VA. I saw that coming, so I had to take what I could get. When I came to myself,

Antoinette was waving her hand in my face saying, "You look as if you were daydreaming."

I smiled and said, "Sometimes that does happen." After saying that, I said, "I will take the place. It will be adequate for me."

Antoinette said, "Remember, if you have any problems with the apartment, please let me know right away. Oh, Samuel, that $50 dollars- forget about it. I will take care of it. Don't be irritated about it." After that, she shook my hand, then gave me the keys and said I could move in as soon as possible. I gave her the money order.

As I left the complex, I noticed there were stores across the street, including a Labor Ready, which was excellent. As soon as I got on the bus, I showed the driver the address 850 Hampton Park Blvd. The bus at that time was completely filled with people talking loudly. The bus driver told me the bus goes near that area.

"Do you know the name of the place you are trying to find?"

I said, "Yes, Resource Consultants, Inc. or as some call it RCI." When I said that, all of the people on the bus became very quiet. When I looked back, I saw nothing but fear and anxiety in the people's faces. It was something I had never seen before. During that time, I looked at the bus driver, he seemed as though he was a little nervous.

I noticed his hands were agitated or should I say shaking on the steering wheel. The people continued to say nothing. You couldn't even hear a pin drop. I asked the bus driver if he had ever heard of the company before. His look was one of concealment, as if he were hiding something. After about thirty-five minutes on the bus, it reached Richette St. The bus driver told me to get off there and go across the street and take the bus straight up. "You can't miss it. Just stay on it, and you will reach RCI."

When I got off, I noticed the people still had that look on their faces. When I crossed the street, I saw the bus arrive. After getting on, there was no one on it. Meditating, I was thinking, *Did I do the right thing giving first month's rent for a place I didn't really like? Should I have spoken with the landlord Betty at Westover Apartments in Arlington, VA and tried to work something out? I have always gotten along with her.* Then, something crossed my mind. I have never had a mind of absence. Instead of seeing my family doctor William Peterson, should I have gone to see a psychologist instead? As the saying goes, 'That's water under the bridge.' When the bus got there, I saw the address RCI 850 Hampton Park Blvd.

As I got off, I looked and saw the building. I noticed the architecture was very strange. When I entered in front, on the left side was the cafeteria, and a lot of people were there. I think it was about lunch time. In the crowd, there was Stephen. He came over and shook my hand and said, "I had a feeling you were going to come." He introduced me to some of the workers there and took me to see Tom, one of the top bosses of RCI. He was the top boss in Detroit, where there was a RCI company there. He was visiting in Capitol Heights, MD. We shook hands and talked a little before he asked me where I was from and said, "You sound like you have a southern accent."

"My father was born in Rockingham, NC, but I was born in Washington, DC," I said.

Then, he responded, "My parents and I are from Greensboro. I will put out a good word for you. Do believe me, you will be working here."

After John left with the other bosses, Stephen said, "You have impressed one of the bosses already. That's pretty good. I got to get back to work now. Lunch is almost over. Welcome to the team. Take care."

When I left the building and stood waiting for the bus, I called Renée and told her that I was in Maryland and was going to stop by to talk with her. Before I could say anything else, I heard a loud voice in the background. I knew right away who it was: Yvonne. I asked Renée what she was talking about.

Renée said, "Sam, you know how Yvonne is." I told Renée to ask Yvonne if she could stay a little longer after 4:00 because I wanted to talk with her.

After that, I said, "Could you stay, too?"

She said, I'll ask Yvonne, and I'll be here when you get here, Sam."

I said, "Okay." When I got off the phone, I started thinking, *Renée has always been there me. Whether things were good or bad, she was there.* Then, I said, "Maybe I got what I deserved." While I was in a deep meditation, it seemed as if it took no time for the subway to get to DC General Hospital. When I walked in, Dr. Peterson and Yvonne were in the back talking about a patient. Renée was at the desk. She smiled as always and asked how was I doing and also my mother and sister.

I responded, "Their doing fine."

Then out of the middle of nowhere, she asked me as she had before, "What is wrong, Samuel?" That time, I stood speechless not knowing how I was going to tell her the news. Then she said, "You have that look of concealment on your face. I can see it."

Then, I said, "Do you think you could take a few minutes off and go to the store with me? I will tell you."

She said, "Okay." As we walked down the hall and then out of the hospital, I told her what happened, except for the relationship with Paula, and how I was going to move to Maryland and start working for a company called RCI. When I said that, she became speechless and would not say anything. Then, she started yelling, "Where are you going live? You know I have six cousins staying with me, and I'm trying to get them on their feet, and now you have gone out to Maryland and found some job and don't even know where you're going to live?" She continued to yell, until I was able to calm her down.

Then, I said, "Renée, listen. I forgot to tell you that I did find an apartment." When I said that, she looked at me like I was a fool.

"How can you afford to live out there? Where at and how much?"

"Hillside Heights Apartments, and the rent is $449 a month."

She said to me, "You have lost your mind. There is no place that can be that cheap, unless it is the kind of place that is inferior. Is that what it is?"

I said, "No, it is not small at all."

Renée said, "Samuel, no place could be in good condition for that price. I would like to see it."

"Well, I don't know about that."

"Then, let's go. It is past fifteen minutes already." As we were on our way back, I told Renée that I wanted to talk with Yvonne to ask her if her brother could help me move. "You must be kidding. Her brother stays drunk all the time."

When we got there, Dr. Peterson was already gone, and Yvonne looked as if she were ready to leave. Then, I said, "Yvonne, I have something to tell you," with a big smile on my face.

She said, "Don't be joking with me, boy. I am ready to go home."

I said, "I'm moving to Maryland."

She responded, "What did you say? Wait a minute. Did you say you were going to move to Maryland?"

"Yes, I did."

When I said that, she put her hand on her side and said, "Do you know what the hell you're doing?"

I respond with a smile, "Yes, I do."

"I would like to see this place," she said. "How are you going to move your things out there? Have you talked to anybody about helping you?"

"No," I said. "That's why I want to talk to you. Could you ask your brother Mike if he would help me move? I will pay him."

She said, "You know you are going to need a truck and someone to drive it. I will do that for you, but I want to see how the place looks. It must be in the ghetto area." After hearing that, I said to myself, *She's right.* Yvonne continued, "I will talk to my brother, but I have a cousin who can help also."

I said, "Sister Yvonne, I've been knowing you for some time. How much is this going to cost me?"

"Well," she said with a smile, "I have to rent the U-Haul truck and pay for gas and the time my brother and cousin take to move you, so usually $250. But, I will charge you $200 instead."

I thought that was pretty high, but I said, "Oh, well. Okay."

She said, "I'm giving you a good deal. Sam, we have to move your things from Virginia to Maryland. Do you have the money now?"

I replied, "No. I spoke to Dr. Peterson about paying you. He will take care of it tomorrow."

I looked and Renée had a strange smile on her face, as if to say Yvonne was going to keep most of that money for herself. When we left the hospital, I asked Renée if she was coming with us. She said she had to check on her grandmother before taking off.

She said, "I hope things work out for you."

Yvonne said, "It will. He's with me." Yvonne had always been bossy but also had a sense of humor. As we got in the car, she turned on the music, listening to her favorite singer Barry White. As she turned the music up, Yvonne tried to sing, but it just was not working.

She looked at me and said, "I can sing, can't I."

I said, "I think you're great."

Yvonne looked at me with a smile and said, "You're the first person that ever tell told me that in my life." I have told some lies but who hasn't? But that time, I told a big one. As we got near Prince George County, which is in Maryland, before I knew it, Yvonne had picked up speed, trying to get past the light before it changed. But, she didn't make it. As we waited for the light, I was thinking to myself, *She really believed me when I told her she could sing.*

Before the light turned green, a car pulled up beside us. The guy that was in it seemed to be intoxicated and absent. While waiting for the light, Yvonne sang louder. The man yelled out, "You need to practice your singing, lady. You sound awful!" She looked at him and told him to go straight to hell.

"Oh, and you need to fix those crooked ass teeth you got!" When the light turned green, she took off like she was in a race or something.

I came right out and said to her, "You need to slow down or else you are going to run over somebody."

"That's not going to happen. I've been driving like this for years on this same road. The Prince George County Police knows when Yvonne is coming to get out the way. The road belongs to me!" When she said that, I just smiled and shook my head. When we got to the apartments, I was thankful there was no accident from the velocity she was going. When we got out, Yvonne looked at the apartments and replied, "These are not as bad as I thought. I'm glad you got one in the front of complex where the office is."

I said, "I got something to tell you, sister." I have always called Yvonne that because she was like a second sister, and she and my real sister got along well.

She said, "What are you trying to tell me, Samuel, that you didn't get a place here?"

I said, "No, that's not it."

"What is it?"

I start to mumble.

She told me, "Stop the bullshit. Get to the point!" Finally, I told her I didn't live in the front of the apartments.

"Then, the second building?" she asked.

I replied, "No."

"The third?"

My answer was, "No."

"I'll be damned! The last building in the back?" I nodded my head. "Then, that's the reason it was cheap. Because the last building in the back of the complex looks the worse!"

When she said that, I started feeling a little ambivalent, asking myself if I had rushed into it too quickly. But as the saying goes: "That's water under the bridge." I have to deal with it, not Yvonne.

She said, "Are you going to show me the building?" As we walked down to the building, she had an expression on her face as though she was very disappointed in me. That's what hurt me the most, as if she were trying to say, "Samuel, you could have done better than this." But, I didn't show my feelings of hurt. The saying, "Sometimes you have to laugh when you feel like crying," is a true saying.

When we got to the apartments, which was the fourth complex, Yvonne's eyes looked as if they were straight up. Then, she said, "Oh, my God." A few minutes later, she said, "Let's go in." When we went inside the building, down the stairs and into the apartment, I was amazed at how clean and nice it was inside. Everything looked brand new when I saw it. It was adequate for me. When we left out, Yvonne said, "Well, it looks nice inside, and you've got a roof over your head. That's what matters the most."

After she said that, I asked her to drop me across the street, but before she said anything else, she told me she would take me to Addison Station where I could catch the subway. "Be ready tomorrow. Me, my brother, and cousin will be at your place at approximately 10:00 a.m. to start moving your things." When we got to the station, I gave her a hug and thanked her. She told me, "Don't worry. Things will get better in time. It will work."

I smiled and said, "They will." I got on the blue line, which was the line that went all the way into the VA area.

Although it was going be a pretty good ride, it would give me some time to meditate on the things to come once I moved to Maryland. I knew that the state was going to be different and so were the people. It would be a new community, learning how to get around, and making new friends or at least trying to. When one moves to another state, it can make the individual feel as if he or she is moving to another country. When the subway got in the Washington area, I started to stop at DC General to see Renée, but then realized it was 4:30 pm. By the time I got there, it would be past 5:00 pm, so I continued to stay on the train. We passed by Virginia Rosslyn Station first; then, we passed through two more. Last but least, we arrived at Ballston Station.

When I got off, there was a rush of people going upstairs or entering the escalator. I made a left turn, heading for the mall to get a bite. As I entered in, I looked and noticed there were many people in the mall, especially at the food court. Then, I said unto myself, "Today is Friday- payday for most people, mainly here in Virginia, who work downtown in Washington, DC." As I waited in line for my order, I looked around at the innumerable amount of folks that were there. Then all of a sudden, something struck me like lightning. Where will I stay tonight? That is what crossed my mind. The waiter that was getting ready to take my order somehow was reading my mind and said, "There is a shelter at 540 Wilson Blvd."

When she said that, my eyes opened widely, and I said to her, "Thank you very much."

She responded, "You're welcome."

I took my food and walked around, trying to find a table to sit at. The more I moved around, it seemed as if there were more people at the tables than it was when I was in line for my order. The louder the voices became, the harder it was to understand what the people were really saying. Then, out of the middle of nowhere, there was a small table and chair all the way in the back. I rushed to get it before someone else did.

When I sat down, I took a deep breath and said, "Thank God." As I took my sandwich in my hands and was ready to take a bite, a thought crossed my mind like an eclipse: It was about the shelter the lady told me about. Although I lived in Arlington, VA, I didn't know there was a shelter there. I had heard of the location of the street it was on, but I said in my mind, *I will find it and stay there tonight. I can't go back to that apartment for even one night. I would have a nervous breakdown.*

When I came to myself, I looked and noticed my plate and cup were empty. I looked around, and some of the people in the food court were gone for the day. The maintenance came up to me and said, "You must have worked hard today. You tore that food up, man."

I smiled saying, "It was a hard day on the job," knowing very well I was lying. As I got up and left the mall, I continued to say to myself, *You can do this. You can do this.* I guess everyone is cautious his/her first time staying in a shelter, not knowing the people or what it's really like. When I crossed the street heading to Ballston Station, where the buses and Subway were located, I looked and saw one of the metro supervisors helping what looked like foreign tourists. I'm not for sure if they were or not, but the way their voices sounded and the clothes they wore made me think so. I stood there and listened to how he talked with the people. He had to have an open mind to talk with them as they asked questions.

I went up to him and said, "Pardon me."

He said, "Yes, can I help you?"

"Yes, I'm looking for this address." I showed him the piece of paper I had the address written on, but I did not put the word 'shelter' on it.

He looked at the address and said, "I know this place." My eyes stood when he said that and out of nowhere, he said as loud as he could, "That is a shelter where homeless people stay. Take the 38 bus. It will get you there in about an hour." The way he yelled out, every person who was in that area looked at him. He looked at me smiling and saying, "You better get there as soon as you can. They serve at 7:00 pm." I looked at him in a strange way as if to say, "How do you know that?" He gave the piece of paper back to me and left. As I stood there waiting for the bus to come, I thought to myself, *The 38 bus goes downtown in Arlington before crossing over going into Washington, DC. I have been in that area many times before but never saw a shelter down there or the name of that street.*

When the bus pulled up, I got on it, not wanting to ask the bus driver. I thought unto myself, *I will find it some way or another.* As I rode the bus, I heard a couple of men saying they were going to have a good meal that night because Mrs. Johnson was going to be doing the cooking there. One said, "You know the line is going to be long, especially for seconds." Once he said that, I knew without a shadow of a doubt he was referring to the shelter. I was quiet on the bus, looking out of the window but still watching them to see what street they were going to get off at. As the bus reached the downtown area of Arlington, the two men got off as I did. They crossed the street on the left side. I stood at the spot I got off at, to make it look like I was waiting for another bus. When they crossed the street and went a little ways down, that's when I crossed. They made a left turn.

When I got there, there was a shelter mission at 540 Wilson Blvd. There were many people in line. There were many tall, small, young, old and just about any race you could name, including sex of both male and female. As I got in line, one man asked me, "Have you been here before?"

I said, "No."

He said, "Then, go up to the front and tell them that you are new and this is your first time." As I began to walk up, I looked and was surprised to see the humble looks on all the people's faces, as if they were thankful to get something to eat and a place to lay their heads that night. When I saw that, it really hit a nerve in me, but why? I do not know all the people in this world we're on called Earth, not even all my relatives. But one thing I do know that never crosses anyone's mind: Growing up, we never think one day we would be in a shelter. This thought was on my mind as I got up to the front.

When I got there, one of the workers said to me, "How are you doing today, sir?"

I said, "Okay. This is my first time here."

He responded, "Then, follow me." As he led the way, I looked and was very impressed with how clean the men and women's areas were. I noticed how the beds in both areas were spotless, as well as the restrooms. They looked like they had never been used before. The shelter looked like it was brand new and was getting ready to be opened for the first time. When we got into the office, he told me to sit down. Then, he asked me my name.

I responded, "Samuel D. Webster."

He shook my hand and said, "Samuel or Mr. Webster? Which one do you prefer to be called?"

I said, "Samuel."

He said, "Samuel, my name is George. What brings you here and how can I help you?"

I decided to tell him what happened five years ago when I locked myself out my apartment and had to stay at a shelter two days in Washington, DC. I made my story sound as if it happened two days ago. He asked how long I had been homeless.

I said, "For two days."

"What were you doing those two days?"

I replied, "Riding the bus, stopping at the Ballston Mall, walking around, then going to Pentagon City, and hanging around."

"Where did you sleep those nights?"

"I got on the subway and went to Washington, DC and got off at Union Station and went to Greyhound Bus Station on 14 St. NE."

"Did they let you stay there that night?"

"The first night they did. The second night, one of the workers told me a van would be there at approximately 12:00 that night to pick up some others and me." I began to tell him the story of the other shelter I had gone to before when I met Mr. Johnson, even though it happened long ago.

I said, "As Mr. Johnson was getting ready to walk away after telling me about the van, I said, 'You said others.'"

He smiled and pointed to the other side and said, "You see some of the people sitting down? Not all of them are waiting for the bus but some for the van like you, to take them to a shelter or church to stay for tonight."

I was in a complete shock when he said that. Why? Because every person sitting on the other side was wearing what looked to be new clothes and shoes. As I sat there trying to figure out which were homeless, a call came through on the loud speaker. The ones who were waiting for the bus going to New York City got in the front. As the people got up and left, there were ten still sitting down. As I looked up at the clock, it was 11:55 pm. Within seconds, a man came in and yelled, "Shelter bus! Get in line!" Everyone including myself got up and got in line. As I turned around, I noticed I was the last one. As the line moved, he asked everyone his or her name. When he got to me, he asked me my name. When I told him, he said, "You are new."

I replied, "Yes."

He said, "I'm used to seeing the same faces every night. That's why I ask."

Once everyone was on the van, some seemed a little agitated or absent, as if their minds were not there. As we rode around from street to street, the shelters we stopped at were filled. They had an overflow. Mr. Johnson, who was the van driver, told us, "Not to worry. I will find a place for all of you." As we continued to ride around, we finally came to a Catholic church. It looked as if the people that lived there had been there all their lives. When we pulled up, a nun came out.

Mr. Johnson greeted her and said, "How are you doing, Sister?"

She responded, "Good as always, Brother, and yourself?"

"Well, Sister. I need your help." When he said that, the nun turned around, looked at the van, and saw the men on it. Then, Mr. Johnson said, "Sister, I don't want to be a burden on your shoulders, but they have nowhere to go."

She smiled and said, "That's okay. The guard is working at the church tonight. I think I can help you, but I don't know if there is enough room for everyone."

Mr. Johnson replied, "If there are two or three left, I think I can find something for them." Then, he asked all of us to get out the van and stand as he called our names. When he called names, the men advanced. As the line got shorter, it looked as if everyone was going to make it in until he got to the last person, which was me.

The nun looked at Mr. Johnson and said, "I'm very sorry. We are out of space, and there are no more beds." When she said that, Mr. Johnson tried to reason with her by saying, "Sister, is there any way at all that you can find a space for him to sleep on the floor and put a blanket down for him to sleep on?"

The nun replied, "We have rules and governance here, and we must go by them." When she said that, she seemed so ambivalent about it. But when she was finished talking, I looked and was astonished when I saw what looked like a tear coming out of the nun's eye. She seemed as if she was trying to hide it by smiling. I went over to her and hugged her and said, "Thanks anyway." Mr. Johnson looked at me as if he was ambivalent about it.

He said to the nun, "Thanks, I will be here 7:00 in the morning to pick them up." When he said that, she replied, "God be with you and brother Samuel tonight. You will find a place to sleep tonight."

When we got into the van, Mr. Johnson took what seemed to be a deep breath and said, "I know one of the volunteers at CCNV. I'll see if there is some way he can let you come and stay there tonight." When he said the name of the place, I thought of a person named Mitch Snyder who fought for the homeless people in DC. As Mr. Johnson got on the phone and spoke with the volunteer he knew, whose name was Ed, they talked about the jobs they work on and how it was going. Mr. Johnson replied, "Look, I have a big favor to ask of you. I have a person that needs a place to stay tonight. I just came from the Catholic Church on 450 N.W. It was filled, but I was hoping they could take one more. But, the nun told me the church goes by rules and governance."

Before saying anything else, Ed said, "Bring him over. I will find some room for him to lay."

Mr. Johnson said, "Thanks, man. I owe you one. Thanks. Peace." After getting off the phone, he told me, "He is going to let you stay there." Being tired and sleepy, I was glad to hear him say that, but when getting there, I found out Ed did not give all the details on the phone to Mr. Johnson about what to expect. When we pulled up, Mr. Johnson shook my hand and said, "I hope everything works out for you." He seemed as if he wanted to say something else but was hesitant. Inside, I noticed the lights were a little low, as if they were about to give out. I saw a man walking down the hall, and I asked him what room Ed was in. "He is in room 105, on the left side." When I got down there, a man I took to weigh over 300 pounds was sitting at the desk and guess what he was doing- eating what looked to be a box of doughnuts with a big cup of coffee.

When he saw me, he said, "Can I help you?"

I said, "Yes, I'm Samuel. Mr. Johnson just dropped me off."

He responded, "Sign the paper, and you can go to your spot. It is in the back on the left side. Your blanket and pillow are back there." As I was getting ready to walk back there, the amount of people was alarming. There were some sleeping on beds but also on the floor. Some looked like they needed assistance. As I was getting ready to take a spot, I looked down and what I saw made me sick as hell. There they were right in front of me- rats and mice. One man, who was on one of the beds, looked at them and said, "They are part of the shelter. They need a place to stay, too." He turned over with a smile on his face. After I saw what I had seen, I was completely devastated. I said to myself, "No, I can't sleep here tonight." I turned and walked away. As I prepared to leave the building, Ed said something to me I will never forget.

"Son, I know this is not a great place to stay, but it is almost below zero tonight. If you stay out there, you will freeze to death." Then, he said, "Look, if you decide you want to come back, I will hold your space." I thanked him; then, I left out. As I walked down the street, not knowing where I was going or where I was going to sleep that night, one of the strangest things happened that I have never been able to explain. As I continued to walk, I looked and saw how everybody that was walking that night had heavy coats, hats, and gloves. Looking at them, it seemed as if the wind was blowing at great velocity. And, they were agitated because of it, but I felt no wind nor was I cold.

An elderly lady walking her dog came up to me and said, "What is wrong with you? Are you not cold?" To this very day, I still cannot explain this phenomenon about how it happened and why I was the only one that was not cold that night. It was unexplainable. I stood at the bus stop, waiting for the bus to come, regardless of where it was going. When the bus came, the driver looked and spoke as I got on, but he did not ask why I wasn't wearing something warm. He seemed like a good person. As I sat in the back feeling depressed, I closed my eyes trying to meditate or should I say rest my eyes. Before I knew it, the bus driver came to the back and shook me telling me, "It's time to get up and get off." As I got up and was getting off, I was thinking and decided to ask him if he knew where another shelter was other than CCNV. He said, "Yes, go down two blocks to 2400 Sixth St. NW and catch the bus going up to the shelter called Benjamin Banneker Community." As I walked to 2400 Sixth St., I looked and there it was- the famous Howard University, the institution that has been the pride of a lot of African Americans.

I waited for another bus, hoping that time something good would come out of it. When the bus came, I got on, praying that the shelter would not be like the other. One thing I didn't know about that city called by many the political and most powerful city in the world was that people do walk the streets and ride the buses late at night. I completely paid attention to the streets. The bus finally came to the Benjamin Banneker Community for the Homeless. When I saw it, I said the words you hear at least one person a day say, "Thank God."

I got off the bus and crossed on the left side. Inside, the man who was at the desk was more professional at his job than Ed. He asked me to sign my name. Then, he asked if I would like something to eat and drink. I did. When he got back, he had with him what looked like a TV dinner. He took some water and put it on it and heated it. Just like that! Completely instantaneous. My eyes went straight up. I had heard of those dinners, but that was my first time seeing one. The military uses them all time. When I finished, I looked at him. He could tell I was going to ask for another one.

He said, "That was the last one. You can lay on any one of those cots in the back." I got up and headed to the back to lie down and go to sleep. Immediately, I looked and just couldn't believe what I saw. There was hardly anyone there. There were 40 cots there, and only two people were there. I looked to the side where the restroom was. I went in there to use it, and everything was clean. I was dumbfounded and a little confused, asking myself, *Why would some of the guys stay at the CCNV in an unclean environment when they could be here where it is more adequate and decent? Is it possible they never heard of this place before?* I couldn't let that remain on my mind. I lay down and went to sleep. How long was I out? I do not know. Then the unexpected happened! I felt as if someone threw a bucket of hot water on me! When I arose, I was in a ball of sweat. It was so hot in there. I felt like I was stupefied. I went to the man who was running the shelter, whose name I never asked.

I said to him, "I'm not trying to complain, but is there any way you can turn the heat down just a little."

He replied, "That's impossible." I looked at him in a very angry way. He noticed and said. "Look, bro. You may have been wondering when you first came in here why there were not a lot of people in a clean shelter like this. Well, this is the reason. The reason is the heat. The city is the one that turns the heat on at 9:00 every night and won't turn it off until 7:00 in the morning. The few people that stay here every night, I let them go out and stand for a couple of minutes. I'm getting ready to call them to come out now."

When he went to call them, I noticed there were four people there that were not there when I came. While standing getting some air, the other guys came to take a smoke break. After it was over, we all went back in. I did get a little air because when I sat down, I was cold. When I lay back down to enjoy what little time was left, as soon as I closed my eyes, it was time to get up. The lights in the room came right on.

The man said, "Fellows, rise and get in line. I got hot oatmeal and coffee for y'all this morning. It may not be a lot, but it's something. I would have bought bacon if I had a couple of dollars on me. I will see what I can do this evening for tomorrow." When I left the shelter, I was thankful. I did get some sleep although it was just a little bit.

George said, "That story was very alluring. Come with me. I will show you your cot." When I got up and went with him, I was still astonished that the place was located in a nice environment in downtown Arlington, VA, not too far from the Pentagon. The cot that he showed me was located in the middle of the room. Then, he said, "This one is yours. Try to keep it clean. Dinner will be served in about fifteen minutes."

When I sat down, I looked around and all of a sudden, I started having déjà vu, as if I had been there some time in my life before. While I sat talking to myself, the rest of the people came in. When the guys sat on the cots, I noticed it looked like they had slept on the same ones, and everyone had his private cart. The ladies' room was located not too far from us.

Being in a shelter is something that we as people in society never dream of it happening to us. That's the reason why I'm not going to reveal their names, to respect their privacy.

The guy that sat next to me shook my hand and said, "You are new here."

I replied, "Yes."

Then, he said jokingly, with a smile, "Welcome to the club." As the other guys sat, they waved their hands and spoke. The ladies in the other room stood up, looking and smiling, as if they were trying to see who was new. Everyone there seemed as if they were in their right state of mind. George came into the room and told everyone to get up and get in line for an unknown reason.

I was feeling happy, as if everything was going well and I had nothing to worry about. There were three ladies in the back cooking. Even before getting halfway up there, I knew what we were having chicken, mashed potatoes, and greens. When I got up there, I noticed the demeanor of the ladies; they seemed to take their job very seriously. Although it was a shelter, before getting the plate of food, one of the ladies asked me for the ticket.

I said to her, "George did not give me one."

Her response was, "Come on. You got that ticket. I saw you when you put it in your back pocket before you got in line."

When she said that, I jumped, "Madam, I swear I didn't get a ticket. Ask George. This is my first day here. He never told me about a ticket."

She looked at me with a kind smile and replied, "It's okay. I was just playing with you." I took a good look at her and could see the leniency in her. I could also see what distinguished her from the other two. She told me, "If you want seconds, it's here." It seemed like the shelter emphasized special attention, which a lot of homeless people need, especially when they are down on their luck.

The chicken, mashed potatoes, and greens hit the spot, as we southern folks say. Before I knew it, everyone got up and got in line for seconds. They did that instantaneously. When I got my seconds, I once again thanked her for her hospitality. She wasn't the type of lady that you had to try to win over. You only needed to show her that you were serious about changing your life, and you would have her support.

As the guys and I started on our second plate, she came over to us and said, "Can I get a favor from you fellows?" Before I could open my mouth to respond, one of the guys yelled out loud, "Sure." Then, he said, "Can we get a yea or nay on this vote?"

Everyone answered, "Yea."

Then, I said at approximately the same time, "How can we be of assistance to you? Just name it, and we will do it."

She said, "The other workers had to leave because of a emergency. I need some strong men to help me clean up around here. Can y'all do this as a big favor for me?"

Before she could say anything more, everyone including myself got up and began taking the trash out, moving the tables and chairs around to sweep the floors, and putting everything back in place. While we were working, George came in, saw us, and was very impressed at our performance. He seemed as if he was unable to articulate what he wanted to say, but he managed to say, "Good job, fellows." As we were cleaning up, we were talking and laughing, but mostly joking, trying to enjoy ourselves and be thankful for what we did have. The ladies, on the other side, got into the conversation by saying, "Work faster. Time is important." We all had a ball, I felt something I had not felt in a long time: happiness.

Then, I got quiet and questioned myself saying, *Is it normal for a person who is homeless to be happy?* Within a flash of light, an event happened. I don't know what it was. I felt as if I was a descendant in a complete world of quietness where nobody spoke or talked, but I remained in silence. Whatever that was that happened to me, whether it was daydreaming, meditation or a seizure, the timing of it in my mind seemed to have been two hours or even longer. But finally, a voice came through. I had heard someone say, "Samuel, are you here, bro?"

I responded, "I am. What's up?"

"We thought we had lost you," he said. "You were out for about five minutes." When he said that, I was somewhat puzzled because of the timeframe he said. To me, it seemed to have been longer. When the lady came back and looked around, she completely smiled then clapped her hands saying, "I had a surprise for all you fellows here and ladies as well for next week, but because of the excellent job that all of you have done, I will give it to y'all now."

We all stood still with a smile on our face. Most of the people there in the shelter, men and women, had known the generous lady for some time. From what they told me, some had known her for one year, some longer than that. They said, she had always been the same kind person. I had just met her, but for some reason, I felt as if I had known her all my life. She left the cafeteria for a couple of minutes. When she returned, she told all of us to follow her, which we did.

After getting in line when we got into the room, our eyes opened widely at what we saw. It was as if it were Christmas time. On the chairs were our names. The chair with my name on it was in the middle. This great lady had for us on the table gifts and cake and ice cream. Like many times before, she was demonstrating her kindness. All the guys, including the ladies, and I were inarticulate about how thankful we were to have a person like this, especially when we were homeless.

People had walked by us without looking as if we didn't even exist, and here this lady, with the kindness of her heart, stepped into our lives when she didn't even have to do it. If God would ask me today to name five people I think deserve to come into my world, this lady without a doubt in my mind would be one of the five people.

As we continued to eat and enjoy ourselves, the lady came in with a DVD in her hand and said once more, "I need to ask a favor from all of you. Will y'all watch this classic movie with me? It is what my family and I in the past used to look at before they passed away. As of this day and time, y'all are my family."

When she said that, I became ambivalent with the feeling of joy but also of sadness. The name of the movie is *It's a Wonderful Life* (1946), with James Stewart. After she asked us, George came in and said, "Fellows, I hate to say it, but is time to hit the sack." After saying that, he noticed the strange look on all our faces. He asked us what was wrong.

The lady responded, "George, I know in a shelter there are rules and regulations, but is there any way you can break them just this one time?" When she said that, he looked as if he was ambivalent.

Then, he said, "What are you trying to say?"

She answered, "When I was growing up, my family and I would watch this movie all the time."

He replied, "What movie is that?"

She said, "*It's a Wonderful Life.*"

George said, "That's the same movie my mother and father used to have us watch."

She then said, "I know it's a long movie, but I would love for the guys and ladies to watch it with me."

George said, "Although we have rules and governance here, and we have always gone by it, there's a first time for everything under the sun. I will go ahead and do it for you, but I don't want to make this a habit."

The lady looked at him as if she were about to cry. Then, she said, "Thank you very much."

George responded, "You are welcome." Then, he said, "Oh, what the heck! Instead of y'all getting up at 7:00 am, I will make it 9:00 a.m. because it's going to be a long movie." We all jumped for joy when he said that. As I turned around to smile at the lady, I noticed she would be in the room, but all of a sudden she would be gone but would return without anyone seeing it. Only angels can do this. I started wondering if the lady was really an angel in human form. I was in a way kind of comparing.

While I was in a deep thought, I felt a hand on my back. When I turned and looked, there she was with popcorn and soda that she had gone to get.

She said, "Are you okay, Samuel? You look as if you were in a world of your own."

I responded with a smile saying, "Sometimes, I am."

She then said, "Come with me."

I know I missed some of the movie, but what is a movie without snacks? When we went back in, I noticed how deep the people's minds were on the movie, as if they were giving it their full attention. When she said, "Popcorn and soda," everyone jumped for joy and got up to get it. With both women and men present, why did I say the ladies name first? Because they were served first. We all sat and looked at the movie, while eating and enjoying ourselves, not knowing the heartbreaking news we would hear the next day. We all laughed and talked, even while looking at the movie. There is a saying when one or many are enjoying themselves: Time moves fast. And, that it did.

It was 7:00 am. This type of time progression had happened to me before- when I was in my apartment one night. When the movie was over, the lady stood up and said, "Can one of you go out and get George? I have something to tell all of you."

I said unto her, "I will." Before getting up, I had the strange feeling that we were about to get news that would not be good for us. As I gathered the people in the room, it was silent for a minute while she stood in front of us, as if she were saying a prayer.

Then, she said unto all of us, "I love y'all very much, and I always will. The news I have to tell all of you is that I will be leaving for another job in a different state. This one pays."

After she said those words, every one of us had mixed feelings: one was joy because she was getting a job that pays, but feelings of sadness knowing that we would be losing her. As I was about to say something, all of a sudden, George broke down in tears saying, "I will truly miss you." When he said that, I turned my head back, trying to keep the tears from coming down. We knew for the shelter to get another volunteer like her would be hard to do, especially someone the people love dearly. The lady went over to George and tried to comfort him, as she did for all of us. I thought to myself, *I would not want to discourage her because she deserved a better job.* I understood where she was coming from because I myself was getting ready to move to another state and was getting ready to start a new job for a company that was doing well in its business.

The lady said unto all of us, "It is almost 8:00 o'clock. Could you guys do a big favor for me when the shelter closes? Could y'all help me move my boxes into the truck? I will treat all of you to dinner."

George responded, "Say no more. We would all have the honor." All of a sudden, I almost jumped out of my skin. I had to pack my own boxes!

The lady said, "Which restaurant would you like for us to go to?" When I looked at the guys, as well as the ladies, they had, as we say in the south, a 'shit look' on their faces as if to say, "Why are you asking only him? Why not all of us?"

I was unable to articulate how I had to quickly get down to where I was living, to meet Yvonne, her brother Mike, and cousin. I was late. Oh boy was I late! Yvonne was probably at the apartment already going off and giving my neighbors a piece of her mind. I could hear it in my ears then. "WHERE THE HELL IS THAT SAMUEL!" Not only that, but I had the idea that an eviction notice was on my door or my furniture had already been sat outside. All those thoughts were running through my head, as if I were in some kind of trance.

All of a sudden, I heard someone's fingers snapping, and I started blinking my eyes, as if I was stupefied or confused a little. The lady asked me, "Are you okay?"

I responded, "Yes, I think I am." She told me what happened that made me feel like I was in the twilight zone, which has happened to me many times before.

"You were out for almost fifteen minutes." I was shocked when she said that.

I said, "Are you for sure?"

She answered, "Yes, I am," with a serious look on her face. What seemed to me to have been only five seconds turned out to be fifteen minutes.

I asked the lady, "Can we talk in private? I have something to tell you."

"Sure, but try to make it quick."

"You are kind of in the same boat I am. I'm moving to a different state and also will be getting a job. What I have to tell you is I have to go now. I can't help you move because I got an eviction not some time ago, and I'm supposed to meet some friends to help me move. They are probably there now and mad at me for being late. I must go now."

The lady hugged me and said, "You take care now, and I will always have you in my prayers, Samuel." I almost choked when she said that, and the tears came running down my face.

I then asked, "What is your name? I never did ask you the day I met you."

She ignored my question, but said, "To this very day, I can't get out of my mind that we had met before, but it was in a different time and a different life." After saying that, she walked away. I then thought about a book that I once read before called *Old Souls* about reincarnation.

****

As I saw the bus approaching, I took off hoping in God's name I would not miss it. At first, it did look that way, until the light changed. That was one time I was glad to see a red light. As I got on the bus, the driver looked and said, "How are you doing?" Before I could respond, he said, "You look as if you are in a rush to get somewhere. Everybody on here is in a hurry. There was a bad accident. That's why I'm late. Hold onto your seat. I'm taking off at high speed." When I sat down and he took off, I tried to think positively, hoping that if my things had been sat out that Yvonne was there and still waiting for me.

As I heard people talking loudly on their cellphones, it was not easy to understand what they were really saying. I was about to call Yvonne as the bus made the turn on Washington Blvd. When the bus stopped at the light, for some strange reason, I stood up to see how many cars were in front of us. When I did, I noticed Yvonne's car on the opposite side. That's when I went to the front and said, "Pardon me, sir. You might think I'm crazy for saying this, but can you let me out here? I know it's against bus regulations, but I can't miss that car across the street. The lady in it is the person who is going to help me move my things."

The bus driver said, "Sure. I will blow the horn to try to catch her attention." And that's what he did. While I was getting off the bus, Yvonne saw me and pulled the car over. When I crossed the street and got into the car, she said in a low but unrelenting voice, "Why are you late?" She was very angry. "I have been waiting at the apartment a long time. Your used-to-be landlord Betty was putting your furniture and other things out when I got there."

I interrupted Yvonne and said, "She was doing it?"

She said, "No, she had some people from Labor Ready putting your things out. I confronted her and said, 'Can't you at least wait until he gets here?' She said, 'No, I have waited for him before, but still he didn't pay up.' I told her that my family and me were going to be helping you move and that we were waiting for you. I asked her if there was any way we could move your things for you before you got there. Betty said, 'Okay. I'm sorry things turned out the way they did. I told her, 'That's okay. It is what it is.'" Yvonne continued, "I left my brother and cousin at your place to go down to McDonald's to pick them up something to eat."

As we rode to Ballston Mall, she was quiet all the way going down there. She seemed as if she was ambivalent about me. That is what I believed. When we finally got there, she parked the car across the street from the mall. "Do you want something? It is on me."

I said, "Sure." Then, I looked at her face-to-face and said, "Yvonne, I'm sorry for being late. I truly am." She then looked at me and could tell I was sorry.

She then said, "That's okay. But in the future, don't do that shit again. Time is valuable." She also said, "You know that I love you. You are almost like a second son to me. Now, let's go." When we went into the mall, it was jammed pack. People even from the Pentagon went there for lunch. As we stood there waiting, I turned around and looked at the large amount of people that were there. Then, my eyes popped wide open. The table and chair that I had sat at when I was there and the friend who went there for lunch had told me about RCI were still there since I left. Even the cup I drank from was there. It was something I could not explain, not even to myself.

Before I knew it, Yvonne started shaking me, asking, "What's was wrong with you? You sound like you are mumbling or talking to yourself. What do you want? We have to hurry and get back as fast as possible to move your things." I ordered a Big Mac meal. As soon as we left and got back in the car, Yvonne took off quickly. When we got back, Mike and his cousin were laying down in front of the apartment sleeping. Before we could get out the car, the Arlington County police showed up looking as if they were ready to arrest Mike and the cousin, as if they were homeless people desecrating the neighborhood.

Yvonne told the officers, "These guys are my relatives. They are not homeless. We are here to help our friend move his things."

The officers responded, "Okay. It isn't a problem. We were called, and we had to check it out." Yvonne gave them a strange look. We went in, and I looked into the corner where I once saw the spirit form that said unto me in strange low voice, "What are you going to do now, Mr. Big Shot." I started shaking and looked at Yvonne, her brother Mike, and their cousin and said, "Do you smell that?"

Yvonne responded, "What are you talking about, and why are you agitated like that?" She then turned to Mike, and he called 911. "I think he's having a seizure."

I responded, "No, I'm not having one. This is a phenomenon not a myth. Y'all don't smell that?"

They said, "No. What does it smell like?"

I said, "I can't explain it, but it's making me very nervous." I looked to the left side of the wall in the living room where the phenomenon had previously appeared. Even Yvonne, her brother, and cousin saw breathless little drops of water going down the wall as if the wall were sweating.

Mike said, "I have never seen anything like that before." When the sweat reached the floor, it headed to the door. When it left out, the nervous feelings began.

Yvonne then said, "Let's hurry and move your shit out of here. This place is haunted." She looked and told her cousin, "Here are the keys. Go get the U-Haul truck. It is down the street. Sam, Mike, and I will be bringing some of the things down from the bedroom."

As we were about to go up the steps, I stopped and said, "I can't do this, Yvonne."

As she had said to me many times before, "What is your problem?"

I said, "You don't understand." I was feeling inarticulate. Then, I said, "Something took place in that bedroom before in the past."

Yvonne said with a smile, "Okay, player. What was her name?"

I took a deep breath and said, "Paula."

"I bet she was hot. Wasn't she?"

My answer was, "She damn sure was." When we got to the top of the steps and made a right turn, which was where the bedroom was located, Paula's perfume smell was still there. Yvonne was always giving her point of view.

She said, "That was some strong perfume she had on." As we began to bring the things down the steps, Mike said, "Sis, you stay down here and put the things down."

She said, "That's a good idea." The cousin, who went to get the truck, knocked on the door when coming in. Yvonne asked him, "What took you so long?"

He responded, "I had to go get some gas."

"Okay, that's good," she said. "Go up and help Sam and Mike." After getting all the things down, including the books, which were the hardest, and putting them in the truck and hoping there would be enough room and enough gas, my next door elderly neighbor who had been at Westover Apartments since the 50's, longer than anyone else came out and hugged me.

She said, "I will miss you, but I also will be leaving to go back to my home country Ireland. My relatives are coming to pick me up. I wish you the best, Samuel."

"You too, Mrs. Johnson." I will always remember talking with her in the morning and would respect her because of her age. When we got everything in the truck, Yvonne said finally, "Let's go."

Then, I said, "Yvonne, wait a minute. I have to go back into the apartment to use the bathroom." I really didn't need to use the restroom. I just wanted to see if the wall was still sweating.

She then said, "Whatever it is- hurry."

I went in for a few seconds, looked at the wall, then came out. Yvonne was up front behind the wheel. She looked at me and said, "You look as if you have been shedding some tears." I said not a word. When we got to the rental office, where I went to turn in the keys, Betty the landlord was standing there in front of the office talking with someone. When I took the keys up to her, she thanked me then said, "This is Scott. He will be living in the apartment that once was yours." I shook his hand and congratulated him.

He responded, "Thank you." As I was about to turn away, headed for the truck, Betty said, "I wish you all the luck in the world."

I said, "Thank you." Though she said those words, her face showed a different thought. When I got in the truck, we took off, with Mike and the cousin in the car going down Washington Blvd. As we got close to the Ballston Mall, Yvonne blew the horn for Mike to pass over, which he did.

She asked them and me, "Do y'all mind if I stop at DC General to see Renée before heading to Maryland?"

We all said, "No problem," as we passed by the mall. We were headed in the direction of the Claredon Metro Station going downtown in Arlington where their court and other government buildings are located. Before reaching the bridge that crossed going off to Georgetown, in the District of Columbia area, I asked Yvonne, "Could you do me a big favor?"

She said, "It depends on what it is."

I said, "Could you make a left turn, and when you get to the second light, I would like to see the shelter I spent one day at and met some kind people."

She respond, "Okay, but ten minutes and no more, I have to hurry and get you to your destination." She bumped the horn for Mike and the cousin to follow us. Then, she asked for the address.

I said, "540 Wilson Blvd." As we went down that street, I looked to the right where the shelter was and saw the building had been boarded up and a sign had been placed on it, saying they had moved to a different location, but it didn't say where. However, there was a number to call for information. Yvonne then looked at me and said, "Let's go!"

I was disappointed that I didn't get the chance to see the people who meant so much to me. Although I knew them for only one day, it seemed like I had known them all of my life, especially the lady who I considered very special. She meant a lot to me and the other people. I wanted God to always bless her and watch over her. Those thoughts were in my mind. As we went through Georgetown, I noticed a building.

While I glanced at it, Yvonne said, "That building you are looking at is where the famous movie *The Exorcist* was made. Have you ever seen it?" Before I responded, "OH YAH!" she laughed. As we came close to 1600 Pennsylvania Ave, it was blocked off.

"I'm going to drive around," she said, "until I hit Union Station. Then, I will know where I'm going." As she drove from one street to the next, we finally reached Eastern Market, which is famous in the DC area for its foods. Last, but not least, we reached DC General Hospital. Then, she said, "I'm going let you out here. Tell Renée I will be in when I park." As I went into the hospital, I ran into Dr. Peterson, who was getting off.

He asked me, "Have you thought about what I said?"

"I sure did," I said.

"Keep that thought in your mind," he said. After shaking his hand, I went in the EEG room where Renée worked and asked her how she was doing.

"Fine," she said. "I'm getting ready to do a patient. How are you doing and have you moved into your apartment yet?"

My answer was, "Negative."

"Just say no," Renée said.

When Yvonne came in, I asked, "Where are Mike and your cousin?"

"They are outside talking," she said.

"Renée, give me your address. Sometimes, when I'm not working on Saturdays, I will drop by," I said.

After Renée and Yvonne talked a little, back on the road again we went. Yvonne said to us, "After we move you into the apartment, then when we can go and eat." We all agreed. We got onto Marlboro Pike, which is down from Benning Road. Yvonne said to me, "Maryland is my state, and you have been wanting to move here. Now, you finally got your prayer answered."

Yes, what she said was absolutely true, but I wasn't thrilled about where I was going to live. "We are here," Yvonne said. "I'm going to let you out here, so you can go up to the office and get your keys."

When I got up the steps, Antoinette my landlord said, "Welcome to the community. Here are the keys, and if anything breaks or if you have a problem, let me know right away. I will have it fixed instantaneously. There are a few papers to sign, but you can do that tomorrow."

I said, "Okay." When we both came from the building, Yvonne was still in the truck at the same spot. Antoinette went up to her and said, "Glad to see you again."

"You too," Yvonne said. Then, she said, "Watch over my brother while he's living here."

"I will by all means necessary," Antoinette said. Suddenly, they both burst out laughing. When we got down to the last apartment building, I felt glad to get that apartment at that price, seeing that it was Maryland not North Carolina.

People in both states are totally different. The people in Maryland were pleasant and asked if they could help with bringing the furniture and other things in. I said, "No, thank you."

They responded, "If you need anything, let us know."

"That I will do," I said. I gave the keys to Yvonne, as she went down the steps and turned left. There it was Number 105, the place that would be my next apartment. As Mike, the cousin, and I started taking my things in, I still was wondering if it had been a good idea to take the apartment, especially when it was in a bad environment. I didn't have to start work at RCI until next month (believing that my friends would put in a good word for me). I knew I didn't have a lot of money to rent a better place but should I have at least tried to find one or rent a room? But I was there already, and I had to deal with it.

"Are you talking to yourself again? Yvonne asked.

"We all do it some time."

When we got everything in the apartment, she asked, "Where do y'all want to go eat?"

"McDonald's," I said.

Then, Mike and the cousin said, "Burger King."

Yvonne said, "The vote is 2 to 1 for Burger King." We got back on the Marlboro Pike. A few blocks down from where I lived, there was a Burger King. After parking, we went in to eat. All of a sudden, Mike and the cousin started talking very loudly.

"That's what I want that BIG MEAL, that BIG MEAL with everything on it."

Yvonne said to them, "Shut up! Y'all acting like cavemen who have never been to Burger King before!" I started laughing, and do believe me, at that time I needed something to laugh at. When we got our food, we all sat down to eat. Yvonne and I started talking.

She told me, "I know where you're living at you're not crazy about it, but it beats living on the streets. I checked the heater in your apartment; it is good."

In Prince George County, it can get really cold in the wintertime, and it was almost in the middle of December. "Now, Sam, what are your plans for Christmas?"

"Well, I'm going go to Dale City to my mom and sister's place."

"That's great," Yvonne said.

After we finished eating, we got in the car and went back onto Marlboro Pike, the street that played a big part in the four years I lived in Prince George County, MD. Once we were back at my apartment, I thanked Yvonne, her brother, and cousin for their help although I had to pay them a good amount. After shaking their hands, I asked the cousin his name. When he told me, it was hard to say. Even to this day, I still can't say it.

Yvonne said, "Remember, if you need something, let me know right away before it's too late. When she said that, she kissed me and told me, "Get in there." When I got out the car and said goodbye, I went into my apartment or should I say my new world. As I sat on my sofa, I started going into deep thought again, saying to myself, *It's going to work out. It's going to work out.* One thing I was happy about was across the street was a Labor Ready. I could go there for the couple of days before Christmas and try to make a few dollars.

I called my mom and sister and gave them my new address and told them I would be there for the holiday. They asked how the place looked. I was silent for a few seconds. Then, my mom said, "You don't like it. I can tell."

"It's okay for a start. If everything goes right, I will try to find a better apartment, maybe in Forestville, MD."

She said, "Take care of yourself, and I will see you when you get here for Christmas. And, remember what your father and I taught you and your sister: When things are not working out the way you want them, always remember there is someone worse than you."

I said, "Mom, you are so right."

She then said, "Lay down and get some sleep. I will talk with you tomorrow. I love you."

"I love you too, Mom," I said.

When I got off the phone, I took a quick shower and looked at TV for a few minutes as I began to close my eyes. I dozed off and went into another world or dimension. I dreamed of what happened in the summer of 1972, when my mom, my sister, and I visited our grandmother in Medina, OH. Daddy didn't go because he had to work. We traveled on the Greyhound Bus for the first time. I can really remember it. Although there have been other times, I don't remember them. When getting there, the apartments that Grandma lived in were once occupied by a military base. The architecture of the building looked like it was built back in the 20's. It was hard to tell the front from the back of the apartments. Grandma would always sit in a chair, looking out the window, where there was a large tree down the street or should I say road. Aunt Dee Dee, her son Frankie, and Deborah Ann her daughter lived on what looked like a small hill. By the apartment were some swings and a huge truck that belonged to Uncle Blue. That summer was a great time that I will never forget. Beside that tree was a dirt road and large electric wires surrounded by a gate. Down the road were a stop sign and a gas station on the far right side. The apartment building looked more like a trailer home that had rooms. However, they were actually apartments.

During that summer, my sister, my cousins, and I, other than Frankie and Deborah Ann, would always play outside on the grass under that tree. But, there was just something strange about those abandoned rooms or should I say apartments that caught my attention. When Grandma was in the kitchen making us lunch over on the other side, I would look through the window to see just how it looked. The living room looked as if nothing had been moved for months or even years. While standing there, as if I were in a trance, I heard Grandma coming to the door. My cousins had just got back from Aunt Dee Dee's place. When Grandma went out the door, she said with a loud voice to Frankie, "Where is Sam?"

Frankie pointed to where I was standing and said, "There he is, Grandma." I had just opened the door of the apartment, which was not locked. Before I could walk in for an excursion, I heard my grandmother calling my name and saying twice, "Don't go in there. Don't go in there." But still, I went in.

The apartment had a smell as some apartments do. Not a bad smell, but a smell similar to a brand new book. As I walked around the living room, I started getting more and more anxious, as if my hair were standing up.

All of a sudden, I jumped up out of my bed and started breathing hard. I walked around wondering where I was, not really not knowing that I was at my own place that I had moved to the day before. I sat down on my sofa and began saying to myself, "I got to get myself together."

Welcome to the Family

The alarm clock went off. I ate some cereal and washed up a little. After putting my clothes on, I went across the street to Labor Ready and spoke with Tina, who was in charge or should I say the boss of the company. She told me that I would have to take a short test that was easy and would take about twenty minutes.

"Are you busy?" she asked.

"No."

"Can you take the test now? Then, I will send you out with the rest of the guys, so you can make a little money."

I said, "Yes." After finishing the test, I sat down with the other guys waiting. Then, I thought to myself, *Starting over in a new environment where I had to move to would require getting used to the people and the music playing.* The one thing that I was pleased with was the location of the stores. They were right down the street, in walking distance.

I heard Tina saying, "Get up, guys. It is time to go out. This is your assignment. At the first apartments off Benning Road, the sheriff will be waiting for y'all. Some people are getting evicted, and the owner of those apartments needs help taking out or throwing out some items. When she said that, my face dropped because I was evicted myself in Arlington, VA.

One of the guys asked, "Tina, are the people still in the apartment?"

"I don't know."

Another guy said something that drew the attention of all of us. "What if one of those people have a gun and don't want to leave?"

"That's why the sheriff will be there when y'all get there." As we got in the van and left, I kind of felt ambivalent about it all, but there was nothing I could do about it. When we got there, it was as Tina said. The sheriff was there with the eviction notice. He told us to follow him up to the third floor. As we did, some of the guys had a nervous look on their faces, including me, not knowing how people would react when told they could not live there anymore. It was wintertime, and the news could be very devastating.

When the sheriff started knocking on the door, the owner was beside him with us behind him. There was no response. Then, the sheriff put one hand on his gun and took the other hand and told us all to step back. After we stepped back, he opened the door and nothing at all was there but a piece of paper that had on it: "We moved last night! LOL!"

When we all saw that we didn't have to put anyone out, we were all relieved. Then one of the guys said, "Will we still get paid? I'm going to call Tina and tell her about what happened." The sheriff said we would be paid. We all got into the van and took off, flying to Labor Ready.

Tina said, "I want to see all of you here tomorrow about the same time. I will be sending y'all to a big company, and there will be a repeat ticket for about a week or so before Christmas."

"What company are you sending us to?"

Tina said, "Does it matter? Y'all will be paid. Isn't that the most important thing about it?"

One of the guys said, "Yes, but I want to know what I'm getting myself into."

She took a deep breath and said, "Some company called RCI, located in Capitol Heights, MD. When she said that, my eyes almost jumped out. The guys started asking one another if they had ever heard of that company before. All of their answers were the same-No. Then, one of the guys was getting ready to ask me.

One of the guys said to him, "He's new here in Prince George County. He probably doesn't know anything about it either."

With a smile on my face, I said, "I don't."

"Be here at 7:00 am," Tina said. "You live right across the street."

When everyone left out, they got on the bus and took right off. I went down the street to Popeye's for a bit. While eating, I starting doing what I have always done- go into deep thought or should I say meditation. After I was finished, I went home and started washing my clothes. While I was in the laundry room, one of my neighbors from Apartment 102 came to take her clothes out the dryer. She and I had a little conversation.

She said, "I know you are new here and getting used to it. It will take some time, but if you ever need anything, let me know. I heard the other neighbor tell you with that cheese smile on his face that he would help you with anything. But don't ask him for nothing because he will be at your door everyday asking you for something. My name is Rhonda. I have been here for almost five years, and I have been saving my money because I have plans to move to Atlanta, GA next year. I speak to people, but most of the time when I get off work, I stay to myself. I can tell you are that way, too."

I said, "How can you tell?"

"Oh, do trust you me. We women can tell. If you don't mind me asking, what are your plans for the future? I know you aren't going to live in an environment like this all your life."

"True, true," I said. "The company I will be working for will pay enough that I can save my money and probably move to another complex here in Prince George County, but my real plans are one day to move to Los Angeles, CA."

She said, "Remember, whatever you need, let me know." Before I could ask her if she was single, she said, "I'm not seeing anybody," with her eyes wide open. I start laughing. Then, she said, "I'm serious, not anyone at this time. Maybe some time, we can go out for dinner."

I said, "That would be great."

She then shook my hand and said, "Hope to see you around," with that smile on her face. She then left. As I continued washing my clothes, I said to myself, "This isn't turning out as bad as I thought. I'm going to start working at RCI early although it is through Labor Ready. At least, I will have a permanent job with them next month at the start of the year, plus I have met an attractive woman who sounds like she is serious about meeting a good man." I smiled while talking to myself and saying, "That good man is me!"

After I finished washing my clothes and drying them, I went back home, sat down, and said a little prayer. Then, I put on my pajamas and went right to sleep. Before I knew it, it was another day. My alarm clock went off at 6:00 am. Thank God! I tried to shake off the little sleep that I still had on me. When I did, I ate some cereal, watched TV, then left out to go across the street to Labor Ready. Before I left out, I saw Rhonda in her car going to work. When I arrived at Labor Ready, all the guys were there, except for the driver of the van.

Tina said, "I'm going give him a call." When she picked up the phone, he walked in and said, "Yes?" Then, after giving him the name of the person we would see after getting there, she gave him the address of RCI and said to all of us, "Try to do your best. It's a repeat ticket for about two weeks there."

We all said, "We will." I yelled out the loudest. When we got in the van and left going down Marlboro Pike, making a left turn, still not knowing where we were going. The driver asked a Metro bus driver at the light if he could tell him how to get to 850 Hampton Blvd. in Capitol Heights. The bus driver told him to follow him on

Central Blvd. to the McDonald's, then make a right and go down the street. Then, we would see that address.

"Cool! Thanks," he said to the bus driver. After getting down Central Blvd. and making the turn, we then knew we were not too far from RCI. Then, the driver of the van told all of us that he was going to stop and get something to eat. We still had twenty minutes before we were to meet the supervisor there. So, we all agreed ten minutes to eat, no more than that. When we went inside Subway and were waiting to order, I looked to the side and saw some guys sitting down eating with uniforms on, with three letters that said RCI. Some of the guys were saying to the driver of the van, "Go over there and talk with them and see what you can found out about the company."

He responded, "Hell, no! I prefer to wait until we get there and talk to the supervisor. As we began to eat, the employees of RCI got up to leave out. One of the guys said, "Bye," to see how he would respond, but he said nothing. The driver of the van said, "That's the reason why I said wait until we get there." After finishing eating, we left and got in the van. It took about five minutes before getting to 850 Hampton Blvd. When we got there, everyone looked at the building and became ambivalent about it.

It looked like a building from the movie in Buck Rogers in the 25th Century. I said to myself, "It if looks like this on the outside, I can only imagine what it looks like inside." When we pulled up to the visitor parking area, the driver of the van told all of us, "Do your best." When we went through the main entrance of the building, the cafeteria was in the front, and some employees were still eating. When Bruce the supervisor came in, he shook everyone's hand and said, "I will be back when the cafeteria is clear, and I can talk to all of y'all while sitting down."

I looked, and there was Stephen. He came over and shook my hand. He said, "Tom got your application in the office. I heard him talking with Bruce about how you would start working next month here permanently. I got to get back to work." When he left, the guys looked at me with a very strange look, saying to me, "What was that all about?"

I said, "I know him. We attended the same high school."

"That's not what we are asking you about." they said. Before I could respond, Bruce came in the cafeteria and looked at all of us and said, "Welcome to RCI. Before talking with you about the two weeks y'all will be working here, I will give y'all a tour." After saying that, he said, "Samuel, I would like to see you before you leave."

I said, "Okay." The guys gave me that strange look again. As we continued to walk, I saw some people that I had met and said, "Glad to see you again."

The guys said, "You know these people?"

I said, "A little."

One of the guys said, "I believe you know more than what you are saying."

As we moved further down the building, I looked at the other guys, and we all were very astonished at what we saw. RCI had big computers and a power plant that looked just like the ones from the Batman series from the 60's. Bruce then took us to the back where the mail trucks came in and said, "I will let some of y'all work back here tomorrow to see how y'all do." As we continued to walk through the building, a couple of employees were coming from the opposite direction, as if they were getting off work.

One of them came up to me and said, "Samuel, how are you doing?" I looked and smiled but was uncertain of how she knew my name.

I said, "I'm doing fine and what about yourself?"

She said, "Great." Then, she put her hand on my shoulder and said, "My name is Tina," with that smile on her face. "I'm glad to meet you." I felt something strong going through my body. Then, I was silent for a moment. The other ladies grabbed her.

They said, "Let's go."

When they left, Bruce said, "Are you ready, Romeo?"

I said, "Yes."

After the tour, we went back to the cafeteria, and Bruce said, "If y'all do a great job, there is a chance some of you can get hired permanently in March when we will be passing out applications. Meanwhile, I must get back to work." he then raised his thumb up and said, "Good luck to all of you." Just when he was about to walk out, he said, "Oh, Samuel. I want to see you in the office. There are some supervisors who want to talk with you. I will see that you get a ride back home." One of the guys threw up his hands.

Then Bruce said, "Let me say this loud and clear. Samuel will start working here next month permanently. Why? Because he filled out an application sometime ago. Now, if any of you have a problem with that, say something."

The guys said, "No." And, the one that had thrown his hands up apologized.

I said, "It's all good." The driver of the van congratulated me and said, "You are lucky but also smart, Samuel. You know how to talk to people."

I said, "I learned a lot from my father."

When I went into the office, there was Tom with my application. He said, "Welcome to the family." Then, he introduced me to Cindy, who later would become my supervisor and close friend. Also, I met Dorothy, one of the supervisors, and Michelle, who was in charge of human resources; she was the kind of person who did not bullshit. Tom said, "Tomorrow, come to the office, and I will show you the film on RCI." After finishing the conversation with Tom, Bruce asked me where I lived. When I told him, he said, "Cindy, Dorothy, and David all live in the opposite direction." He was about to call a cab, but Tina came in and said, "I left my cellphone on the desk somewhere in here."

Bruce said, "I found it and knew it was yours because your name is on it. I will be back. I'm going to the lost and found room to get it." When he left, Tina asked me about my application and asked if they had talked with me about working there.

I said, "Yes."

She said, "Are you from the south, Samuel? You have that accent."

I responded, "Yes, I am."

Then, she said, "I love those kind of men."

"Why thank you, Tina," I said. Bruce came back and gave Tina her phone.

He then said, "Do you pass the direction were Samuel lives going home?"

She said, "Yes, I do."

"Could you drop him off? I'll give you twenty dollars." He looked at me and said, "Samuel, you do know that's going to come out your first check." I laughed, but it did.

When we left the company and were driving down the street, we made a turn on Route 45. We were in Forestville. After a couple of blocks, we entered District Heights where the trouble got started. Tina was telling me how long she had been working for RCI and how she had her ups and downs with them. Just before I could open my mouth, I saw a flash of light. I turned my head, and it was the Prince George County police, who in the past and to this present day have bad communication with minorities. They pulled us over, and before we could open our mouths, one of the officers flashed the light in Tina's face and said, "I want to see your driver's license now." Then, he shined the light in my face and said, "I want to see yours too."

When I told him I didn't have a driver's license. He said, "Your damn picture ID. I know you have that."

In an aggressive way, I said, "Yes, sir," with a smile.

He responded, "You think that shit is funny? How would you feel if I lock your ass up? Do I make myself clear?"

When I saw he was not playing, I said, "Yes, sir," in a serious tone. When he took my ID, he went back to the police car and sat down in it for a few minutes.

Tina asked me, "Do you have any warrants on you or records?"

I said, "Hell no."

When he came back, he gave Tina and me our ID's. Then, he told Tina to sign the papers. She looked at me; then, she looked at him and said, "No."

He responded back to her with anger, saying, "WHAT THE HELL DID YOU SAY?"

She said, "I'm not going sign these papers, officer, because I was not speeding. I will go to court and fight this."

The police officer became very furious and said, "That's fine with me. I'll see you in court, and we will see who will win."

After saying that, he got in the car and left. Tina took a deep breath and said, "Let's go."

I said to her, "I am very sorry for this happening."

Tina looked at me. "It's not your fault."

I then said, "If it wasn't for me needing a ride, this would not have happened."

She said, "Don't say it like that. I have been ducking the police for some time for speeding, but this time I wasn't." After getting me home, she asked, "Is this where you live, Samuel?"

I said, "Yes. I know it isn't all that, but it's somewhere to live."

She then said, "I tell you what I will do. Tomorrow, I will come and pick you up at about 3:00 pm. Will that be fine?"

I said, "Oh, yes. How can I thank you?"

Tina said, "Don't worry about it. You can pay me on your first check."

I was about to hug and kiss her, as if I were hungry for something to eat. But, I controlled myself and shook her hand. I really believe she knew that and how I was feeling about her that night. She said, "I will see you tomorrow, Samuel."

I said, "Okay," and got out the car. I went down the steps to my place and sat down for a minute. The guys and I had been at RCI almost all day, but the time had gone by quickly.

Back into Chaos

It didn't take too long before the next day came. As I was taking a shower, I heard a knock on the door. When I went out and put my clothes on, I started looking at TV thinking to myself about what to do until Tina picked me up. Then again, someone started knocking. I started saying to myself, "Who is that knocking the hell out the door?" I went and opened the door without seeing through the eyehole whom it was.

As I opened the door, it was Rhonda, with an aggressive look on her face. "The next time I come and knock on your door, Mr. Webster, answer it, so I don't have to come back a second time." Then, she changed her look from aggression to a smile.

I responded to her, "Yes, Queen Victoria."

"You are not funny, Samuel. Well, since we are having this conversation, I will be free this evening, and I would like for you to take me out for dinner, so we can get to know one another a little better." When she said that, I almost jumped for joy, but then I said, "Shit." Then, she asked what was wrong.

I said, "I forgot I have to work this evening. I just got hired on this job." When I said those words, she took a deep breath in anger and said, "Okay, Mr. Webster. Then, when can we go out?"

I said, "I have Fridays and Saturdays off. Which day would be best for you?"

She responded, "Saturday would be better."

I said, "So be it then."

She looked at me strangely and said, "What did you say?"

I said, "'So be it' is a way I sometimes respond back to people." She said okay as if she didn't believe me.

After a little hug, she said, "Your first day on the job will be great."

I said, "Thank you, Rhonda."

After she left, I was still trying to think of what to do before Tina came at 3:00 to pick me up. I started to leave out and go down to Popeye's to get something to eat. Before I started getting ready to leave, I looked to the side of the living room and saw a bag in the corner. I stared at it for some unknown strange reason; then, I shook my head and said unto myself, "Get yourself together. This is your first day on the job."

Then, I went over to the corner to see what was in the bag. I noticed my dirty clothes were in it, which I had forgotten. I decided instead of going to Popeye's to wash my clothes and get it out of the way. While looking through the things I had in my apartment, one thing I didn't have was washing powder. I went out in the hallway to Rhonda's door but saw where she had put a note on her door for the UPS man, instructing him not to leave the box at the door if she was not there but to take it with him, and she would be home the next day.

Going back to my place, I had to think quickly about whether or not I was going to the store and if I would have enough time to wash and dry my clothes before Tina got there at 3:00.

"Oh, what the hell! I'm going to wash them."

I left out the apartment right away, walking as fast as I could to the Safeway. Getting there was not a problem, but the lines were unbelievably long. I went to the back and got in the pharmacy line, hoping I could get it done instantaneously, but one of the workers told me if I was not picking up a prescription that I could not pay for anything in that line. Instead, I would have to go to the front to pay for it. I told her how I had just moved to the area and my first day on the job was that day and I wanted to wash my clothes before one of the workers picked me up at 3:00 o'clock.

With a smile, she said, "I'm going to give you a break. You can pay for it here, but remember this line is only for prescription pick ups."

I said, "Thank you very much. I will bring my prescriptions here the next time."

She alluringly said, "That will be great. Have a nice day."

I said, "You too."

Leaving the store, I saw some people at a distance make a turn in the woods. I found out later that was a short cut to the back of the apartments. When I got home, I saw some people coming out of the laundry room with their clothes. As soon as I got in my apartment, I rushed to get my clothes and head over. When getting there, I was in luck. Nobody was around. When I put my clothes in the washer, I was hoping they would wash quickly. Then, I left out. Before getting back to my place, I saw what looked like a police officer, but it was a security officer with a gun. I introduced myself to him and told him I was new there and was washing my clothes.

He said, "Welcome to the community."

After having a little conversation with him, I asked him, "Has anyone's clothes been stolen from here before?"

He told me, "Don't worry. I've been on this job for five years. No one's clothes have ever been taken." I was glad to hear those words.

Once I was back in my place, I started putting things in place: chair, sofa, books, and the table. By the time I got it done, I went back to the laundry room and put the clothes in the dryer. It didn't take any time before they were dry. When getting them out and going back to the apartment, as I was folding them up, I heard I loud bumping outside. I knew it was Tina. As I dropped my clothes on the bed and went running out, there she was.

I told her, "I will be back in a minute." Back in my apartment, I put on my favorite shirt to try to look good my first day on the job. While I still was looking around to see if there was anything I needed to take with me on the job, I heard the horn bumping again. I went out running. I jumped into the car feeling kind of ambivalent but was unable to inarticulate it.

Tina said, "Let's go." She took off heading down in the area where there was only woods and no road. Before I could open my mouth and say, "What are you doing?" or anything else, she turned the car around going in the right direction- speeding towards the security guard that I had talked with. I saw him walking on the left side, as if he was headed to the office. He saw us in the car and yelled, "Slow down! There are kids around this area."

When he said that, before leaving out of the complex, Tina said, "May God, be with us getting there." I looked at her curiously. Then, she laughed and said, "Samuel, I always say those words before going to work everyday."

As we rode down Marlboro Pike, she said, "Things are going to work out for you at this company. The reason? You have a good personality, and you are easy-going and know how to communicate with most people."

I looked at her with a smile and said, "Thank you, Tina, for having faith in me." When we got there, I saw that the van from Labor Ready was already there.

Tina said, "I'm going to let you know something. Although you might already have an orientation and a film you have to watch, don't forget to tell Bruce your size, so you can have your uniform next week."

When I went into the front of the building where the cafeteria was, I saw Bruce talking with the guys from Labor Ready. When I spoke to them, the way they spoke back was as if they had ambivalence. When I went into the office, Dorothy was sitting at the desk and said. "Samuel, how are you?"

I said, "Fine."

She asked, "Tina told you about the file and orientation?"

I said, "Yes."

"I'm going to take you to the back in the room and put the tape on 30 minutes. When it's done, come and let me know."

I said, "Okay." The film started with the work that's done at the post office to working overtime and the pressure that was brought on the workers. They couldn't deal with it anymore. That is what convinced the Postal General to call Resource Consultants, Inc. in Pittsburgh. During that time, the headquarters were located there. The video showed how RCI signed a ten-year lease with the post office. Most of the story in the film was about the work that the employees do, which is the same as how it was done at the post office. But, the film didn't tell the dark side of the company and the business it was doing with others that was illegal.

When the film was over, I went into the office, and Dorothy and Bruce were talking. He came over and said, "Samuel, write down your sizes, and I will have your uniforms next week." When I did that, Dorothy smiled. Bruce said, "I like the way some of the guys from Labor Ready are doing. I will hire a few of them two weeks from now. Don't say anything about it, Samuel."

I responded, "I won't."

Dorothy then said, "I'm going to give you a little orientation since it's only you." She asked me a few questions. Most of them I said no to. After that, it was over, so she took me out to the work area that I would be working at. She told me the kind of work I would be doing, which was demonstrated in the film. Then, she said, "Samuel, one of the most important things is keeping up with the work load. It did not mention that in the film. That is one thing all employees have to do.

That's where the pressure builds up. But the company gives new employees a month before they start there." She said, "The mail bags you will be laying down have to weigh 300 or more pounds. All of the bags the employees lay down have to weigh a different weight before they can be taken out."

When she said that I was devastated, wondering how that would work. Dorothy looked me in the face and said, "You can do it. You are vigorous." Then, after showing me the area I would be working in, she took me to the back where all the fork lifters were and the areas where the mail trucks came in. Later, I would find out there were many things the mail trucks were delivering.

Dorothy said, "Actually, this first day is not a working day, but it is for me to show you around the company. Actually, tomorrow will be your first day working." When going back to the front of the building, I saw Tina, Stephen and Richard. They welcomed me and said they were heading out to lunch. "Would you like to join us?"

I looked at Mary, and she said, "Go ahead. After that, you can head home if you want to. Remember, the real work starts tomorrow. Be ready."

"I will," I said. After Dorothy turned her back and start walking away, Tina gave her that middle finger and looked at her as if she wanted to intercept her job. I knew from there that some kind of disagreement or something happened between them, or it probably was more serious than that. Stephen and David told me, "Before we go to lunch, we want to show you an important spot." They took me to where it looked like it was almost the end of the building and said, "This area is what we call 'going out the back.' This is where some of us sneak out for about fifteen minutes before lunch to go and pick up what we ordered. In this company, you can always observe a piece of paper. It is passed around without Dorothy seeing it, for the employees to write down what they want."

I asked, "How many times has that happened?"

He said, "It has always been frequent."

Tina said, "Are y'all ready? Let's go."

David said, "Don't sweat, Tina. The supervisors are in a meeting now, and they told us we had a extra fifteen on lunch break because they think the meeting is going be long." When we left out, we got into Tina's car. When we got to Capitol Heights Plaza, there was a McDonald's, a Burger King, and a Chinese restaurant.

Tina asked Stephen and David which one they wanted to go to. They looked at one another as if they couldn't make their minds up. Then, Tina said, "Samuel, it's your turn. You are treating me."

I said, "McDonald's."

When we went there, Tina said, "Let's eat inside." After ordering, we all sat down and started eating. Tina said, "Did Tom tell you this company has a lot of family members who work here, Samuel? Stephen, who you have known for years, is my brother. We have the same father but not the same mother." After lunch, we returned to the job and finished our shift. After work, Tina dropped me back off at my apartment.

When I got out the car and went to my apartment, within seconds of opening the door, Rhonda came over and asked me how my day was.

I said, "My bad, Miss Rhonda. I thought at this time you would be sleeping."

"No, at this time, instead of looking at TV, I listen to the oldies but goodies, Mr. Webster." I smiled. She asked, "Oh, are you still going to take me out this week."

I said, "Yes."

Then, she said, "I'm going to let you get your sleep." We gave each other a little hug. Then, she looked at me in an ambivalent way and said, "Who was the lady with the braids that picked you up?"

I looked at her and *almost* said, "None of your business."

When she saw how I looked at her, she said, "I'm sorry, Samuel. I almost forgot we just met. What you do with your life is none of my concern. I'm going to let you go. I know you're probably tired."

I said, "I am."

The next day, I called Renée to see how she was doing. When she answered the phone, she said, "Oh hi, Mr. Stranger. Since you got that job in Maryland, no one has heard from you. Dr. Peterson has been asking about you, to see how things on the job are coming along."

I said, "Pretty good, Renée. The reason you haven't heard from me is I've been working and sleeping. The job pays well, but you will have to work hard as hell there."

"Oh, my baby."

"Renée, that ain't funny."

Renée said, "I'm sorry."

I said, "I got to get ready and catch the bus now. I'll try to give you a call tomorrow. Tell Dr. Peterson and Yvonne I said hi."

She said, "I will. Bye."

Finally, the day had arrived for Rhonda and me to go out for dinner. Oh, my God. It was a day I will never forget. We went to a Japanese restaurant in Washington, DC, downtown in the Adams Morgan area. It is one of the most expensive areas in the District of Columbia, other than Georgetown. We were the only black Americans in the restaurant. The only other people, whites and Asians, treated us with respect. I had never eaten in a Japanese restaurant before, but the food there was great and out of this world. We laughed and talked with one another. Everything seemed to be great. I was enjoying myself more than I thought I would.

All of a sudden, Rhonda jumped up and started screaming and cursing, saying, "This damn food tastes horrible! I'm tired of the shit that's happening in my life!" I was devastated at how she was carrying on.

The owner of the restaurant came and said, "YOU GUYS HAVE TO GET OUT, OR I WILL CALL THE POLICE."

When I tried reasoning with Rhonda, she said, "I will say what I want to say. I have rights according to the first amendment." Finally, she cooled down. Still, the owner told us we had to leave. When we left, she was quiet in the car going back home. When we got there, she took a deep breath and said, "Look, I know you probably don't want to go out with me anymore because of the way I acted at the restaurant. I didn't tell you when we met that I am bipolar." When she said that, my eyes stood up. She said, "Look, I know you're probably seeing someone else. I see a woman pick you up every day. I know that's your girlfriend."

I said, "That's not true. She gives me a ride to work. That's all. You know I don't have a car."

Her response was, "Whatever." When we got in the apartments, she looked at me in a sorrowful way and said, "I'm very sorry I messed your day up." She bowed her head down and went into her apartment. I kind of felt sorry for her.

****

At work, it was my turn to go out the back and get lunch. We had decided on Chinese food. As I prepared to go, Tina called my name.

I just looked at her, and before I could say anything, she gave me the keys to her car and said, "Did you think I was going let you just walk down that dirt road? That's too far." She then said, "Go ahead. I will to take care of the weighing and pallets 'til you get back."

I got in the car and took off down that dirt road, knowing I didn't have a driver's license. Getting to the Chinese restaurant, I saw on the menu every kind of food you could name to order. I saw a lady's head in the far back, and her hair was in braids, but I couldn't see her face. I knew it was a black woman cooking back there.

On the way back to work, my phone rang. It was Rhonda screaming at me. "Where the hell have you been? I haven't heard from you! You haven't even come over to my apartment. You seem like you aren't interested anymore. Is it because of what happened at the restaurant? Why don't you want to talk to me?"

"Rhonda, that's water under the bridge," I said. "I have had other things deep on my mind."

She went off again, saying, "That's no excuse for you not calling or even checking on me to see how I'm doing. After all, I am your girl."

When she said that, I said, "Wait a minute. We are just friends. We haven't known each other no more than four months to be in a deep relationship."

When I said that, she told me off and called me every name but the child of God. When I hung up on her, I looked at the time. It had gone by quickly. I stepped on the gas hard, knowing I was doing about 70 miles an hour. When I got there, I knew the workers were going to ball me out.

When parking Tina's car, I had everyone's order. Once I went into the cafeteria, everyone was sitting there with their arms folded and rolling their eyes at me, but they had a reason to be mad. I was about twenty minutes late when I got back. After giving them their orders and money back, instead of sitting down and eating myself, I went to the office and asked Matthew for a big favor.

He said, "It depends on what it is."

I said, "I went on lunch break at the right time to get lunch for myself and some of the workers. I went to pick the lunch up on time, but I was late coming back with the food. Can you give the workers an extra twenty minutes to eat?"

He took a deep breath, and said, "Yes, but you owe me one. I'm going to give them this extra twenty minutes, but I will not do it again. Are you going to eat?"

I said, "Gene, I'm not hungry. I'm going back to work now."

"Are you for sure?"

"Yes."

He said, "Okay."

****

One payday after work, the employees took a drive to a liquor store. When we got at the store, I looked, and Tina said, "Yes, this is where most of the employees cash their checks most of the time because most of the workers are too tired to get up and go to their banks in the morning. Most of us don't get up until 12:15 or 12:30 p.m. the next day. As you continue to work here, you will understand."

As everyone stood in line, what impressed me the most was how the employees waited for one another and watched one another until everyone cashed their check. I call that teamwork. Some of the workers drank, not soda but alcohol, and I mean a lot of it.

When Tina took me home, I paid her and thanked her as I always did. After paying her, I looked at my check stub again. I was still astonished at the money I made after taxes were taken out. Tina and I had become so close that I knew if I had a problem, she would be there to help me. Tina looked at me and said, "What are you thinking?" Then, she said, "Oh, let me guess. You're going to try to flirt with me, Samuel." When she said that, I smiled.

What Lies Beneath the Surface?

When lunch was over and everyone was headed back to work, Bruce said, "Samuel, your uniform will be here tomorrow. Don't forget to pick it up."

I said, "I won't. Is work over?" I said to myself, "Another day's work is done."

When I got to work the next day, I went into the office, and Bruce gave me my uniform, but when I looked at the name it had on it, Bruce said with a laugh, "We had forgotten your name and had to put a name on it." The name that was on it was Denzel. When he said that, Cindy, Dorothy and the other supervisors started laughing hard.

Cindy said, "Well, Samuel, you do look like the actor."

The name patch that was on the uniform was on it in a way that it couldn't be taken off. Bruce said he could order another uniform but that would take some time before getting it, so I was going to have to work with that one.

As days and weeks passed by, my month of training was almost over. By that time, I had picked up the timing of when to work fast and when not to. During the time of working, I saw so many illegal things being done at the company. Many things were being taken off the trucks and sent to the office.

As the days went on, everyone was working even harder than I had never seen, even me. Finally, one day, Matthew came and told us the contest with the morning shift was over and that he would make the decision the next day about who won. "All of you try to get here early as you can." Everyone left out wondering who won- the morning or evening shift. I tried to get it out of Tina, but she wouldn't say a word. She only said, "Just wait 'til tomorrow."

When the day finally came, I decided to go see Renée. She was working half a day that day, and she would be able to drop me off at Addison Station. When I got to DC General Hospital, it was the same way it was every day: a lot of people, a few doctors, and less patients.

As I sat in the EEG room where Renée and Yvonne worked with Dr. Peterson, Yvonne saw me. She said, "Oh, Mr. Big Time Spender. I haven't heard from you since helping you move to Maryland."

"I have been very busy, Yvonne, trying to impress the big man at RCI."

"Okay, Mr. Webster. But, you still have my number, don't you?"

"Yes."

"Keep in contact with me. You never know. Later down the road, you might want to move to another apartment- somewhere better in Maryland." She was right. When Renée and I were getting ready to leave, I asked Yvonne where Dr. Peterson was.

"He decided to take the day off."

I said, "Oh."

"I'll tell him you asked about him."

When we left out, Renée drove down Minnesota Ave NE. Then, she said, "Sam, if you don't mind. I have to stop at Giant Food Store. I will see that you get to work on time. Tell you what, I will take you there when we come out. Is that okay?"

I said, "Yes." After she parked the car, I looked through the store and talked in my mind. *I haven't been in this store for almost ten years since me, Mom, Dad and Toni moved to Virginia. But, it seems like yesterday when we were here. Everything still looks the same, just new faces.* Renée told me she just had a few things to pick up, and she would be ready to go. As I walked around looking, I went into the soap area. I looked and beheld, Lincoln, my father's cousin, who was shaking his head. He asked how everyone in the family was doing.

I said, "Okay."

"Are your mom and sister still living in Dale City, VA?"

"Yes, they ain't never gonna leave there."

"What are you doing over here?"

"I moved to Maryland, and I'm over here visiting a friend."

He said, "Renée," with a smile on his face. "Right?"

"Yeah."

Before he said anything else, I said, "I got a job at a company called RCI." When I said those three letters, that smile of his face turned to a look of shock. It was a look I will never forget.

Then, he said, "Do you know what you have gotten yourself into? My son works there on the morning shift, and I have tried to get him away from that company. As you know Sam, I have worked for the post office for a pretty good while. I have even offered him a position there. If you can pass the test, I will see that you get a job there where I work."

After the short conversation we had, Renée came to the area and said, "Are you ready?"

I said, "Yes."

Then, Lincoln said, "Think on what I said."

"I will." Then, I introduced Renée to him and said, "This is my cousin."

He said, "Nice to meet you. Sam has told me a lot of good things about you."

Renée said, "Thanks. I try my best to give him the best advice. It was good to meet you."

I told Lincoln, "When I talk to my mom, I will tell her I saw you in the store. And, my number is still the same."

When we left the store, I was kind of quiet. Renée asked me what was bugging me. Then, she said, "You know me, Samuel. We grew up together. You can tell me anything, and I will always listen. My ears are open, and my mouth is closed."

I said, "Okay, my cousin that you met in Giant Food Store threw a hint at me about RCI and told me he had been trying to get his son to leave the company and work with him at the post office. He also said if I take the test and pass, he would get me a job there right away."

Her response was, "I have always had peculiar feelings about that company since you joined it but never said anything about it to you. Samuel, do you think you can pass that test for a job at the post office?"

"I sure will try and study for it before taking it."

Getting into Maryland, Renée said, "Remember, I said I would take you to work? How do I get there?"

I said, "Take the route on Central Ave down to where the McDonald's is on the left side. Make a right turn and go straight down."

When we got there, Holy Moly. It looked like chaos. Some of the workers who I knew by name and some by face were outside in front of the building protesting about some of the workers who got fired. It was a Tuesday. I remember that day well. Some of the employees were saying loudly, "These guys that y'all fired are innocent and didn't do that damn shit!"

Renée said to me, "You got something on your hands today. If you can't call me at lunch break, call me tomorrow."

I said, "Okay."

When I got out in front of the building, the workers came up to me and said, "The guys that the company fired didn't deserve it. What we are going to do tomorrow is walk out and continue to protest for the rights of workers at RCI. Are you for us, Sam or against us?"

RCI: The Secret Organization

"I'm for y'all."

In saying those words, I meant it not only for the rights of the employees but rights for myself as well. But in some way, I was feeling a little ambivalent. When everyone went back in the building and start working, Matthew came out on the floor with a loud speaker and said, "I saw the protest outside, and all of y'all have a reason to be angry and upset, but don't jeopardize your jobs. The investigation is over, and they have found out the ones that left the counterfeit money and whiskey in the restroom. All of you must move on with your lives. I know all of you in here have either families or bills to pay. Losing your jobs would be devastating, but I'm going to let all of you make that decision, and I hope it's the right decision."

He went back into the office. All of us just looked at one another, and it was easy to tell what was on everyone's mind. They were wondering if it was a good idea to walk out or not.

At the end of the day, as I got in Tina's car, she looked at me and said, "As one of the supervisors of this company, I can't walk out with y'all, Sam, if that's what all of y'all are going to do. Yes, I think there needs to be some changes for the employees, but let it come at its own time."

When getting home, as I was about to get out, Tina grabbed me by the hand and said, "Sam, I don't want to see you lose your job. You have won a lot of supervisors' trust since you have been here. No, this isn't the best job in the world, but think, Sam. It does pay good money and while continuing to work there, you can save enough money to move to a better apartment, which you probably already have plans on doing."

I smiled and said, "I do."

Before getting out, Tina said, "Sam, please think on what I said."

"I will do that."

****

When I went into my apartment, I ate a little, then lay down, said my prayers and dozed off. Getting up the next day, I showered and decided to go see Renée. It was not 8 a.m. yet, so I had time to go over to D.C. General in Washington D.C. to see her and get back before 3 p.m. As I left out the door, something told me to call before going over there. Luckily, I did. She had left a message on the machine at the hospital stating she would not be there that day, and someone let me know when I called.

I went up to Popeye's and got some chicken to take with me for lunch. Getting back home, I called Mom and told her about how things went that day. She said, "Stay on that job. There are going to be good days and difficult days, but keep your head up."

I said, "I will, Mom." When I got off the phone, I heard a horn blowing. I would recognize it anywhere. When I went out, Tina said, "Are you ready?"

I said, "Yes."

I got in, and she said, "Another day, another day," as we headed down Marlboro Pike. Then, she said, "Something smells good."

"That's Popeye's Chicken. I have four pieces, and you're welcome to two pieces if you want it."

Tina said, "No thanks, Samuel. Oh, I forgot to tell you. Dorothy didn't say anything to you about it, but she probably is going to make you take an oath that you will not say anything about what's going on in this company." When we got there, Dorothy came out the office and asked me to go with her. Tom was there. He had come to see how things were working out for the RCI there in Maryland. It was as Tina had said. In front of Tom in the office, Dorothy made me take an oath with my hand on the Bible, that I would not tell anyone, not even members. I swore I wouldn't say anything to anyone.

After that, I left out and headed to my station. When getting there, the bags were already there for me to set up on the pallet. Dorothy walked up and down the building checking to see how everyone was doing. When she came to me, she said, "Remember, Samuel, you are still in your month of training. In front of me was a worker named Gina.

She shook my hand and said, "Good to see a new face. If you need any help, don't hesitate to ask me."

"Thanks, Gina. My name is Samuel." I talked to her a couple more minutes; then a forklift pulled up with more bags and sat them there.

The driver said, "Sam, I'm Brian, one of the fork lifters. I brought some more bags here, so you will have enough for most of the day."

As I started working, I did what most people do on their first day on the job. I worked hard and fast, but Gina told me, "Don't work yourself out. Just keep up your pace and concentrate. That's the best way."

When the 15-minute break came, Gina and I headed to the front where the cafeteria was located. I saw James, Richard, and some of the crew sitting talking with each other. When Gina and I sat down and talked, she said, "I have been with RCI for about a year now. The money is good, but the work is hard." After the break was over, all the employees headed back to the floor. Most of the workers were quiet and working, including myself and Gina.

Tina came by and said, "I will see you on lunch break." When she said that, she winked her eye, which was a sign of 'going out the back' early to pick up the lunch. At lunchtime, most of the employees ordered Chinese food, except me because I had Popeye's Chicken and Gina had a salad. Everyone talked and chatted with one another. When lunch was almost over, Bruce came in the cafeteria and said, "There will be a meeting."

****

Gina and I grew closer. There would be times when she would finish before I would, so she would come over and help me. I told her many times, "Whatever I can do for you, let me know." Gina whispered, "Samuel, Samuel." I turned and looked. She had a very peculiar look on her face. She continued turning her head over and over, as if to say, "Come over here." When I did, she looked down in the bag, and behold, there were thousands of dollars in it. I noticed it didn't have that little small mark on it. I learned the game fast. That small mark didn't look like anything suspicious. Gina and others never paid any attention to it. Other than me, few knew what it meant. Someone didn't put the mark on it and brought it out on the floor. I told her I would be back. She looked at me as if to say, "Where you going? I have been here for a year, and this is the first time I've run across some money like this." Before I walked away, Gina looked as though she was agitated a little.

When I went into the office, it looked as if there was a meeting going on with Matthew and the supervisors. Dorothy stood up, came over to me, and whispered in my ear, "We're having a meeting. This better be something important."

I said, "It is."

She said, "Let's have it."

I said, "I have one of the bags with a special delivery. Someone forgot to put the mark on it and brought it out to the floor."

In my ear she said, "How the hell do you know about the bag and what was in it?" She turned and said to Gene, "Boss, I have to go to the floor. Something important came up."

He said, "That's okay. Do your job. Some things are more important than meetings."

When she and I left from the office, Gina and the other employees had that look on them as if to say, "What did Samuel go into the office for and what did Dorothy and he talk about?"

Dorothy said to me, "I'm going to the cafeteria to get a cup of coffee. Y'all continue to work and don't come in there. If you do, I will have to suspend you."

When the employees heard that, they knew she was serious. When we got in there, she grabbed me by the arm and said, "How did you find out about those kinds of bags and the marks on them? Some people that have been here longer than you have can't even tell it from other marks on them."

My answer was, "Mary, my father worked for a company that was a little similar to RCI. He taught me how to tell marks on mail bags and what they mean."

Continually looking at me she said, "I'm going to tell you something you already know about. When you got this job, you took an oath not to tell anyone about the things that are happening in this company. Are you willing to live up to your word?"

My answer was, "By all means necessary." Then, I said, "I need this job to get by. Look, I have and have always had ways like my father. I know what he would tell me to do, 'Keep your mouth closed and do your job, and don't tell what the company is doing'."

Dorothy looked at me and said, "I'm going to take your word for it."

When we went back on the floor, Dorothy was smiling and acting as though nothing had happened, but the workers were cautious. Going back to my post, Gina said, "Is everything okay?"

I said, "Yeah."

She said, "Are you for sure?"

I said, "Yes." It seemed as if as she was trying to get me to say something. From that day on, she continued throwing hints about what happened in the office that day, but I stayed silent.

That night, before it was time to get off, Dorothy came out the office and told me, "I'm going to give you a lift home. I have already told Tina." When she said that, I started wondering to myself, *What is she up to?* When all the employees had left their posts, I stood there at mine, just looking around the building, feeling like I was the only person in a town that had been abandoned. When Dorothy came out the office, she was in a hurry and said, "Let's go."

When we got in her car, she took off as if she was headed for a second job. While driving down that road, I tried to talk with her. The only thing she said was, "I don't talk while I'm driving. We can talk when I get to your apartment." On the way there, I was trying to figure out why she wanted to wait until we got there and what she wanted to talk about. When we got there, she parked across the street from my place, where the laundry room was. Finally, she opened her mouth and said, "I'm going to make this conversation short. There is a position available at the company, and I'm offering it to you." I looked at her with shock.

She said again, "I'm offering it to you. Do you want it?"

I said, without knowing what the position was, "Of course."

She took a deep breath, as if she were angry and said, "That was one of the things we were talking about in the office before you came. I'm going ask you one more time not to reveal the secret things to society that RCI is doing."

"I swear I won't say anything to anyone."

Dorothy said, "The position is a weigher and a floor person. Your job will be to weigh employee's bags, walk around the building to see if the fork lifters need any help. If not, come back and weigh some more employees' bags. Then, take the trash out the box office and supervisors' offices, but not the trash on the floor. The workers will do that themselves before they leave. That's all of it. I'll explain it to you more later on, but for now, I'm going to let you go. Oh, when you come in tomorrow, you will have to sign some papers."

I said, "Okay and thanks a lot."

The next day, I officially received the promotion to weigher. In the office, Matthew gave me the papers to sign. After doing that, Matthew said, "Let's go on the floor, and I will show you the machine you will be using to weigh the bags." As we were getting ready to step out, he said, "I gave your post to one of the workers that used to work at Labor Ready." When he said that, I kind of felt a little ambivalent although I had a new position.

When we started walking down the floor, the employees look at me in a way as if I had been talking about them in the office or if I was able to influence the supervisors every time I went in the office. When we got to the back where the scale was, he showed me how to use it and how it works. Then, he said, "I'm going let you handle it now. Remember, if there's anything you don't understand, let me know right away." He left and went back to the office.

After that, I took the scale and said to myself with a smile, "Let me see what I can do." Thinking positively, I took it up to the front floor. There were twenty posts on the floor, ten on each side. When going up to the employees, I said, "I know you are not finished, but I'm going to weigh your bags anyway." Some of the workers were thrilled about it, but some weren't. They felt I was holding them up. After finishing, I went to the back, and before asking the forklift operators if they needed help, they said, "Sam, there's one extra truck coming that didn't make it yesterday. We need your help right away."

My response was, "Okay." When the first truck rolled up, I had a large amount of boxes with a mark on them that consisted of numbers, which was a code to specify what the box contained. The forklift operator set those boxes at the area by the forklift, not knowing that I was able to distinguish the marks on the boxes. When I picked up some boxes and took them to the area where the others with the special mark were, they looked at me and said, "Why are you putting those there instead of the other area?"

I looked at them in a strange way and said, "Do you believe I know what I'm doing?" They were shocked and looked at me in the same way I looked at them. Their look said, "He knows what's going out here." The other truck got in just when we finished the first. Brother, oh brother, did it have a lot of those boxes with that mark. I didn't know what was in those boxes, but I did know it had a lot to do with acquisition, which at sometimes made me feel a little agitated. As we were taking boxes off the second truck that pulled in, Gene, Tina, and David came to the back.

Matthew yelled out, "What the shit is going on, Webster? The workers up front need you to take their bags to the back and bring them some pallets, so they can start on another one right away. Get the hell up front now! David will stay here and help finish taking the boxes off the truck. Tina, I'm putting you in charge to watch them." That was the first time I saw Matthew snap like that, but later down the road, there would be other times.

When I got up to the floor, a lot of workers were waiting to start another pallet. As I started moving the bags as fast as I could, the workers grew impatient because they had to keep up with their quota. "Thank God, I don't have to go through the same thing," I said to myself. James, one of the employees who had been with the company for some time, came out the middle of nowhere and helped me take a lot of the bags to the back, to put them on the mail truck. When finished, I brought some pallets to them to get started on another. Matthew came and told me to help bring some of the boxes with the mark on it to the office.

After finishing, Matthew said to me, "I would like to apology, Sam, for intercepting you at the truck. I know that's part of your job. As the boss of a company like this, sometimes one has to be solid."

I said, "I understand, Gene."

Then, he said, "As you already know, these boxes that are brought to the office are very important and are brought to RCI on heavy guard."

When I got home, I started thinking to myself, *This job pays good, but what have I gotten myself into? When I joined this organization, did I really know what I was doing?*

The next day on the job, while the workers were doing their jobs, I went to the back and got a large number of pallets and brought them upfront, not too far from where the workers were. The day was turning out pretty good. Tina came up to me and said, "It's almost time to hit the back. Write down what you want for lunch." After doing so, she went to the ones that mostly order. When the time came for her to leave out, something happened in the office, and she had to see about it, so she gave the piece of paper with the orders on it to Rita.

We sat in the cafeteria waiting. Finally, she came back with the orders. As we ate and talked, Gene, Mary, and Tina had a special visitor Tom from Pittsburgh, who was visiting to see how the RCI in Maryland was doing. He said, "I received a report from Matthew on how y'all are doing, and from what was told to me, everyone is doing magnificent and keeping up with their quota. That's the kind of report I want to hear." When Tom said those words, everyone started clapping. After that, Tom said, "Well, I'm going to let y'all finish your lunch, and again, thank you all." We all were glad to hear those words.

Matthew said to me, "After lunch, Sam, come in the office." Richard, Robert, James, and even Gina, as well as all of the employees, started looking at me again with that strange look. Finally, one of the employees who I didn't know that well said, "You know, Sam. It seems like you are in that office a lot I see."

My response was, "Yes, I am, but they are the ones who are telling me to come in the office. I'm not going in there on my own. I'm no supervisor. I'm just a regular worker just like y'all are."

Gina said, "Samuel, I believe you," while the other employees said the same. Once lunch was over, I went in the office. Most of the supervisors were in Gene's office in the back. When I got there, as I stood there waiting, I noticed one of the boxes with that mark on the side sitting by the wall, and it was open. I saw what was in it although it was only open a little. It was moonshine, as we call it in the south. All kinds of thoughts start crossing my mind. *The trucks that brought it there were under heavy guard.*

While I stood there thinking deeply and talking to myself, Matthew came out and said, "We will have another meeting tomorrow in the cafeteria. Make sure you tell everyone when you leave out. From now on when preliminaries are coming up, make sure you inform the employees about it because they probably want to know why you come in the office all the time." When he said that, he smiled.

My response was, "Do believe, Gene, they do."

Before I left out, he said, "Oh, Sam. I know you saw what was in that box, didn't you?" I was silent for a minute. Then, he said, "Remember, you are a part of this organization. If you hang us, you hang yourself as well. Don't forget that." When I left out, I told the workers that there would be another meeting the next day. Before they asked me, I said, "I don't know what it's going to be about."

The next day, more boxes without a mark where delivered. Most of the trucks that came in every day had license plates from California and Arkansas. When the time came for the meeting, it was about twenty minutes before lunch. When we went into the cafeteria, Matthew and the other supervisors were already there, and he had a look on his face as if what he had to tell us was not good news. There were three people with him.

Matthew said, "Look, although Tom and I are very impressed with a great job all of you all have done, and everyone has kept up with their quota, there still has to be a change. These new people will bring that change to the company, and we will be even better. The three new people are Carl, Cindy, and Nancy. These people have been with RCI in Detroit for some time. They will transfer here to show workers how to speed up a little. All of you are doing a great job."

Then, he introduced Carl. First, he said, "I thank everyone here for coming to this meeting. I will show all of you how to work fast without wearing yourself out. Thank you."

Nancy said, "If anyone has questions or issues, feel free to talk to me after." But, then the bombshell came. We heard some news we were not expecting.

Matthew said, "Cindy, here will be your new supervisor. She will replace Mary." When he said those words, it got very quiet in there. You could hear a pin drop. The other workers and I were devastated. We were so inarticulate or should I say dumbfounded. Dorothy had a look on her face as if she were ready to kill someone. Matthew said, "Look, I know none of you were expecting this. Dorothy is a great supervisor, but I feel she would do a greater job in the office instead of on the floor."

Carl was doing a great job, and the workers were working fast, even me. He showed me which bags to weigh first and which ones to weigh last. He was almost like a counselor, someone to talk to about personal problems, but really not problems on the job. Cindy was doing a great job also as a supervisor. She was very quiet at the time, but she was watching everyone, to make sure they were doing their job and reaching their quotas. I noticed a lot of the workers were going to the restroom quite a lot, but I didn't pay any attention to it.

We continued to do a great job, but there seemed to be more stress and tension among us. Arguments broke out and even fights. Some of the employees were suspended. Matthew talked to us, telling us all to calm down. "Don't let your attitude cost you your job." Everyone finally cooled down and went back to work.

When the trucks came in one day, Matthew told me, "From now on, you will only weigh the boxes coming off the truck, but Carl will be the one to bring them to the office from now on."

I said, "That's fine." I noticed when weighing them, there wasn't that mark on them anymore. I saw also there were different boxes coming out the trucks that also had different license plates, not from California and Arkansas. I was a little curious.

When lunch time was near, Tina was nowhere around. It was time to go out the back to pick it up and ask everyone to write on the paper what they wanted. I thought maybe she was in a meeting. When the other workers and I went into the cafeteria, Gene, Tina, Carl, and Cindy, as well as the other supervisors shouted, "Surprise!" They had cake, ice cream, soda, hot dogs, and hamburgers.

Matthew said, "It was my idea to have this party to show all of you how much I appreciate what all of you have been doing." While all of us ate the cake and ice cream, as well as the hot dogs and hamburgers, we all started thinking, *He's one cool white boss.* But, later down the road, we would see the other side of him.

When the other workers and I got to work the next day, we looked and everyone was speechless, except the words that came out of my mouth: "Oh, shit!" There were about ten police cars from Prince George County in the parking lot. We all started looking at one another, trying to figure out what was going on. When we got in the building, Gene, as well as the other supervisors, was cursing up a storm, not at the police, but at some of the employees asking, "Who in the hell left those two bags in the men's restroom?" He was looking at all of us with anger at the time. I didn't know what he was talking about. The police officers had bags in their hands, the bags that the employees put on the pallets. The police yelled out loudly, "Everyone in the damn cafeteria now! That's a damn order!"

Looking at one another, we thought someone was going to be fired. We all went into the cafeteria before Matthew and the supervisors. We still looked at one another, wondering who was getting fired. When Matthew finally came in with the supervisors, he said, "Those police officers that you saw in here, those bags they took with them had $50,000 in counterfeit bills. The other bag had bottles of I don't know what." When he said that, I knew he was talking about the Moonshine Whiskey. "Some of you know something about this," he said. "Those police have put out an investigation on this. Let me tell you this is not the last time we are going to hear from them." When he said that, the workers and I became a little agitated. I didn't know at that time what to believe and who to believe. "You are all dismissed," he said. When that white man left out, his face was almost red.

It was pretty quiet on the floor. Then, things went back to normal. The talking and laughing and 'going out the back' for lunch returned. Then, all hell really broke loose.

One day while I was picking up the bags and bringing in the pallets, four white men in suits, clean shaven, with short hair came into the building. I had that strange feeling all over me. *Oh, my God. I know who these guys are.*

Every one of the workers was devastated as hell. The white men went into the office. Willie, the oldest employee, the one we all looked to when the employees had problems with a supervisor, said, "I will go in there and try to find out what I can." When he went in there, it only took him a couple of seconds before he came out and said, "Brace yourself. I got some shit to tell all of you. Those four white men that you saw go into the office are the FBI." When he said that, every one of us almost had a stroke. He told us that the police had turned the case over to the FBI. After saying that, he went back into the office. We all knew from then on that someone or more than one was in a lot of trouble.

Then, he said, "Just lay back. Keep cool and do your job." As we went back to work, nobody could get out their minds off the FBI, especially when most of the employees were black Americans. The question all of us kept asking one another was, "Did you take that bag of counterfeit money and the other bag to the restroom and drop it off?" There were many workers going back and forth to the men's restroom, but I can't recall ever seeing one of them taking a bag in there. It was a mystery, but when it finally came out who took it in there, we all were totally devastated.

Anxiety only caused us to work faster, but then hell broke loose again. It was not among us in the evening shift, but among the ones in the morning shift. They were leaving trash for us to clean up, and words were exchanged between them and us. Matthew set a new rule that the ones in the morning would clean up their own trash.

Before Tina dropped me off, she said, "There are going be some changes tomorrow. One of them is my timing at work. I will have to be at work two hours early. I will be able to take you home when getting off, but you will have to catch the bus going to work now. Some of the workers catch the 266 bus from Addison Station. I'm sorry about the change," she said.

I said, "You have nothing to be sorry about, Tina. You're still my girl." We both laughed.

Inside my apartment, I ate a little. Then, I paced back and forth until I went to sleep. When I woke up the next day, I took a shower and tried to figure out what I was going to do about the strike. Too many things were going on at work that I was uncomfortable with, from people being fired, to the police and the FBI showing up. I went to Safeway to buy some food. When I got there, I walked up and down the aisles, trying to figure out what I wanted to eat. Then, I ran across some employees from the Coca-Cola Warehouse, and they told me they saw me and some of the other employees of RCI protesting and threatening to go strike a couple of weeks back. They said, "A couple of years ago, we were in the same boat y'all are in, and we knew we were taking a big risk by going on strike, but we knew we had to do something, so we went on strike. When we did that ABC 7 News came by and asked us what the strike was for. When we told them for the rights of the workers of Coca-Cola Warehouse, the Teamsters Union found out and became our union. They can do the same for RCI."

When I thanked him and shook his hand for the information he gave me, he said, "Good luck." As I turned to walk away, he then said, "Wait one minute." He then reached in his wallet and got a card that said Teamsters Union Organization with its number. Once more, I thanked him.

I got my groceries, and as I walked back home, I was thinking about the conversation I had with the employee from the Coca-Cola Warehouse. When I got to my apartment, I was glad I didn't see Rhonda. When I went in, I just sat down, after putting the groceries on the table. I looked straight at the walls. Then, I pulled out the card that the worker from Coca-Cola Warehouse gave me. I said to myself, *I have to call these people; I hope they can help us.*

When I called, the Secretary of Teamsters Union answered the phone and said, "Teamsters Union Organization, can I help you?" When I mentioned my name and whom I worked for, she then said, "We saw you and others employees protesting yesterday as we drove down the street. We did call RCI and set an appointment for you and the other workers to meet with y'all and the supervisors. Don't worry. No one will lose their job."

When she said that, I said to her, "Could you wait one minute, ma'am?"

She said, "Sure."

Away from the phone, I said, "Thank you, Jesus."

When I got back on the phone, I said to the secretary, "Thank you very much."

She said, "You are welcome. We at this organization are always doing what we can for workers' rights."

After I got off the phone, I called Gina and told her the good news. When I did, she said, "One minute, Samuel." I heard her in the background saying, "YES!!" Then, she got back on the phone and said, "Continue, Samuel."

Then, I told her, "We and the Teamsters Union are to meet with the supervisors tomorrow."

She said, "I was almost ready to give up."

We talked for a few minutes more, and I said to her, "Be ready for tomorrow."

After standing outside for about two hours, forgetting about Tina's new schedule, I decided to catch the bus to work. I got on the bus and went to Addison Station, where the employees of RCI hung around before going to work. When I got there, they were in a meeting, talking about the strike.

I said to them, "Are y'all ready for today?"

They responded, "Ready as we always will be." There were many people at Addison Station. Some looked like they were headed for the subway. As we waited for the bus, a lady came by with her son. The little boy looked at us and said some words that I will never forget.

"Mom, aren't those people in those dark green uniforms the people you said work for the Mafia?" When the kid said those words, everyone at the bus station looked at us in a strange way.

"When we get to work, remember we are all in this together," James said, ignoring the little boy's comment. What surprised me was some of the workers seemed like they were with the strike, even if it meant losing their jobs. But some were saying the risk we were taking was just too big. "Why don't we just wait about three months then go on strike?" someone asked. The other workers didn't want to do it that way. After drawing straws, it was a tie. I had the final vote about whether we should or shouldn't. That was not the first time something like that happened to me where I had the final say so, and it made me feel like the world was on my shoulders. I was thinking deeply on what the workers from the Coco-Cola Warehouse told me at the store.

As we continued to stand there, my phone rang. When I answered, it was Renée, asking how things were working out. I told her about the meeting we had with the Teamsters Union the next day and how they were going to do what they could for our rights.

"Things will turn out fine. I will be praying for you."

When I got off the phone, I stood there thinking about the six days we had to work, and if the Teamsters Union could do something about that. Some of us had been working six days for three months. One of the employees of RCI told me the reason for working the six days was because the morning shift worked six days too, and we were competing with them in a contest. When he told me that, I almost couldn't believe it. The winners would get a $500 bonus and that's one of the reasons for working six days. But, the contest had already ended, and we had remained on the six-day schedule.

While I was standing there looking like I was in a trance, the workers said unto me, "Sam, are you for this strike or not?"

Finally, I gave my answer, "Yes, I'm for it." After some of the workers took a deep breath, I said, "Let's get on the bus and go."

As we were walking up to the bus stop, the workers, who were not for the strike and tried to intercept it, rolled their eyes at me.

When we got off the bus and started walking down the street, the cars that were going down the dirt road were bumping their horns at us knowing that we worked for RCI. Once we got to Hampton Park Blvd, I saw all the employees, plus what looked like an organization that had brought sandwiches and bottled water to the employees. Before the volunteers left, they said a prayer.

At break time, Bruce told all of us that in ten minutes there would be a meeting. When he said that, we were thinking he was going to tell us how great we were doing on the job. Instead, we got the unexpected. While waiting in the cafeteria, Bruce came in with Matthew and said, "I'm gonna try to make this story short. I have been hearing rumors of a strike, and y'all have heard the possibility of me taking another job in Dallas, TX, but as of now, that's not the important thing. I'm going to let Matthew talk to y'all."

When he got up, he said, "I had been with RCI for some time before coming to Maryland. I was with them in Pittsburgh. When I was transferred here to the RCI in Capitol Heights, MD and met Bruce and the other supervisors, I made a vow that I would do my best, not only for the company, but for the employees as well. I know that a lot of you are angry and bitter over the employees that were fired."

When he said that, we all yelled loudly, "Yes!"

When we all calmed down, he said, "We are looking into that back in Pittsburgh. We had something similar to this, but we were able to work it out."

James jumped up and said, "Yeah, y'all work it out because the employees in Pittsburgh are white. We here in Capitol Heights are black."

When he said those words, Bruce said to James, "You are suspended for two days now." James sat down with anger in him.

Matthew said, "In some ways, what he said is right. I have heard about y'all walking out tomorrow and going on strike. Think about your families and bills you have to pay."

Although I lived in an inexpensive apartment, I was saving money to move into a better place. I was thinking if we didn't go on strike, any of the workers including myself, could be fired for no apparent reason at all, or we could be treated any kind of way like we weren't American citizens. Or, if we did go on strike, there was no telling how long it would last or if they would get substitutes to replace us and pay them less. It seemed to me that we had all those thoughts in our minds when everyone left out that night.

When I arrived home that evening, I was confronted by Rhonda.

"Where have you been? Look again, I'm sorry. Can we start over?" After she said that, I was thinking about how I was going to get rid of her.

With a smile on my face, I said, "Okay."

Her response was, "That's good. I'm going to let you go now. I know you need your rest." She then shook my hand. When she turned and walked away, I was kind of feeling a little ambivalent about her. Then, she opened the door, turned back and looked at me and said, "Oh, I forgot to tell you, we are going out this Saturday, Samuel." Then, she closed the door very hard. It seemed as if she was doing everything she could to influence me. I said to myself, *This is another problem. But, I have to deal with it later.*

When I got on the bus the next day, I couldn't wait to get to Addison Station to tell the guys the good news about the Teamsters Union. With everything going on the day before, I did not have an opportunity to tell them. When the bus got there, the workers were hanging at the same spot they usually did. They were saying we should continue to strike. When I walked up to them, I was quiet and had a big smile on my face. Finally, they said, "Why the hell do you have that smile on your face, Sam?"

I said, "I got some news to tell all of y'all. Brace yourself. Yesterday, I called the Teamsters Union and talked with them about what is going on and what we are going through. They told me they saw us on the news and would be at RCI to talk with the supervisors and us and not to worry because no one will lose their job."

After telling them what I considered to be good news, they looked at me and started laughing and said, "Yeah, Sam. Right." I couldn't believe how they responded and did not believe me. Before I could say anything else, the 266 bus pulled up. As we started walking to get on it, I was mad as hell. I had good news and after telling them, they didn't believe it one bit.

Light at the End of the Tunnel

When we got on the bus, they started talking about what we could do now that the company was saying they were going to hire temporary workers if we didn't go back to work. As they continued to talk, I didn't say a word. When the bus got to the corner of the dirt road, we got out and walked. Everyone, except me, continued to talk about what may happen.

When we got to Hampton Park Blvd., they looked and their eyes opened widely. The Teamsters Union was already there talking with Matthew and Channel 7 News. The workers looked at me, and I pointed my finger at them, and said, "I told you so." When we got to RCI, there were three people from Teamsters Union. They looked at us, and one of them said, "Which one of you is Samuel?"

When I said, "I am," he shook my hand and said, "Glad to meet you, Samuel. My name is Peter. The secretary told me you called."

When he said that, Matthew looked at me in a peculiar way. Peter somehow noticed it, and he said to me, "Things are going be okay. Don't worry. Trust me." After saying that, he said to us, "I had a talk with Matthew about what is going on at RCI and how there needs to be some changes here. There will be a meeting tomorrow at the Fire Station in Hyattsville, MD at 10:00 am. Now, I'm going to let Matthew tell you the rest."

When Matthew took the microphone, he said, "Thanks, Peter. When I took this job as your boss, I knew from the start there needed to be a change, and I'm glad that it is finally coming now…" After he finished talking, Matthew said, "Well, that's it for now." Then, he looked at Peter and said, "Is there anything else?"

Peter said, "No, I'm getting ready to go. Remember 10:00 a.m. tomorrow." Then, he shook my hand and said, "See you, Sam." Then, he left.

After that, I turned and gave the employees a strange look in their faces. They looked like they were ashamed for not believing me. Before one of them could say anything, I said, "It's all good. Don't worry about it." We went inside the building and started working as if it were the first day at RCI. When lunchtime came, we went to the cafeteria as usual and sat down. No one had lunch with us because of the strike. Tina came in and had coffee and donuts with her. She gave it to us and said, "Congratulations. I'm glad something worked out."

When she left, we all started talking about the meeting that would take place the next day. Then, David said, "It's going to be at the Fire Station in Hyattsville, MD, but where?" When he said that, before anyone else said anything, I called Teamsters Union and got the location: 6200 Belcrest Rd. After everyone wrote the address down, we went back to work, after eating the donuts and drinking coffee.

As I weighed the employees' mail bags, I was thinking about some of the questions to ask the next day, like how quotas were bringing a lot of pressure on the employees because they didn't want to lose their jobs and how sick employees could not take off without being fired. As I was thinking about those things, before I knew it, there was some chaos. Some of the employees on the morning shift came in saying they wanted Sam to be the speaker for the employees of RCI when the Teamsters Union became our union. I had heard of one of the employees named Sam on the morning shift, but I had never met him.

The employees on the evening shift, including me, had already made up our minds that Bruce would be the speaker. As we began arguing with one another, the situation escalated and was getting deep. Gene, Tina, and Dorothy came running out of the office saying, "What the hell is going on out here?"

The others and I from the evening shift responded first by saying, "We made our minds up that Bruce would represent us, while the morning workers said Sam will."

Matthew said, "None of you are going to make that decision." After Matthew said those words, everyone backed off.

When Tina dropped me off at home, she said, "Let me say this, Sam. Remember, you didn't hear it from me. Y'all are going to get something in the meeting, but not everything." Tina had a peculiar look on her face.

I said, "Okay. See you tomorrow."

When the next day came, I did a little jogging. Then, I went to Washington, DC, to see Renée, how things were coming along, and what Dr. Peterson was up to. "He's seeing a patient now," Renée said, "and Yvonne is doing an EEG on a patient." I asked Renée if she would like to go to the cafeteria, so we could talk.

She said, "Sure, let's go."

When we were on our way there, I told Renée the news about Teamsters Union and the meeting at the Fire Station and said, "This is what we've been waiting for a long time, but my mind keeps telling me something is strange behind all of this."

Renée said very loudly in front of everyone, "Stop thinking negatively. Put that to the side and think positively. Things are going to work out, Sam. You will see. Trust God."

When we finished eating breakfast and had gone back to the EEG room, I told Yvonne, who was finished with the patient, "I might need you again."

She responded with a smile. "Really?" she said.

"You were right, Yvonne. I have been saving my money since working at RCI to move to another apartment."

Yvonne said, "Where is the apartment that you are interested in?"

I said, "Doral Apartments in Forestville, MD."

When I said that, Renée said, "Boy, those apartments are sky high in rent because they are across the street from the mall."

Yvonne said smiling, "Don't say anything, Renée. Sam is making big money at RCI. He can afford it." Renée had that smile on her face as she always did.

Then, I said, "I'm getting ready to go. Tell Dr. Peterson I will see him next time."

Renée and Yvonne said, "We will tell him. Take care."

Then, Renée said, "Let me know how things turn out."

Then, Yvonne said, "My turn. When you are ready to move, let me know something."

I said, "I will. Y'all take care."

Leaving out, I called Gina and asked her if she was already at the fire station. She said no because she was on her way to Addison Station to meet up with some of the other workers. They had decided to go together. "Where are you, Sam?" she asked.

I said, "I'm about to get on the subway at Stadium Armory Station."

She then said, "I will tell the other employees that we are going to wait for you."

When I got off the phone, I jumped on the orange line, then next on the blue one. Before I knew it, I was at Addison Station. Mostly everyone from RCI was there but quiet and wasn't talking too much, which was kind of strange. When the P12 bus pulled up, we all got on, but some of the employees had to wait for another bus, which took about ten minutes. But, we all still got there at the same time. There were many employees at RCI who had their own car, so they drove on their own.

I tried to start a conversation with the other workers, but the way they responded was as if they were nervous about how it was going to turn out at the meeting. That was on my mind, too. When we got there, I didn't even have to look out the bus to see if we were on the right street. The fire station was so large that a person could see it five streets down. When we got off the bus and looked across the street, there were many cars parked in front of the fire station. The workers from the morning shift were already there, also. Tom, Gene, Cindy, Mary, and Bruce were there. Those of us from the evening shift were wondering why Bruce had not shown up at Addison Station.

Matthew came up to us and said, "We are going to wait a couple more minutes to see if anymore are going to come. Then, we will go ahead. We have some coffee and donuts. Help yourselves."

While eating, Bruce said, "I'm sorry I didn't come to the station." Then, he started smiling and showed us some keys. He had bought a car earlier that morning. Then, he said, "Now, let's talk about this meeting. First, I'm going to say that I would like for us to get everything we want. Unfortunately, y'all know that's not going to happen. I'm just glad we are finally getting a union."

"When it's your time to speak let them know what we need to work for this company," James said to Willie.

When we finally went in, Peter spoke first saying, "I want to thank you for showing up here. Teamsters Union has always been here, from the days of Jimmy Hoffa. We are a vessel for the workers who feel the companies they work for are not treating them fairly. We as Americans have rights, even when we are working for a company that is making millions upon millions of dollars and is owned by millionaires. Some of the workers feel that nothing can be done, but that's where we the Teamsters Union steps in for the workers." When he said those words, we all stood up and applauded.

Then, Matthew went to the microphone and said, "Thanks, Brother Pete," with a smile on his face, "for that speech you gave. I would like to say sometimes things can happen. At first, you don't understand why, but later down the road, you will understand why it had to happen the way it did. And, that's why I'm wondering why the employees took a chance and went on strike." As Matthew was speaking, a piece of paper was being passed around. When it came to me, it had writing on it that said, "Sam, if you and the others don't vote for the Teamsters Union, all of you will be...?" The thought was incomplete. It only had a question mark instead of the rest of the sentence.

When I read what was on the paper, I grew a little agitated. I looked around to see if anyone was watching, but everyone seemed to look normal. When voting to see if we wanted Teamsters Union as our union, many of us voted for them. When the counting was over and they became our union, Matthew shook Peter's hand and said, "Welcome." We all stood up again and applauded. Then, the next step was to determine who would represent RCI and be part of the union: Bruce or Sam?

Peter said to all of us, "I have spoken with Tom about who would be the best man for this position, and I want to say both employees have been with RCI for some time and have done a great job for the company, but as you know, we can only choose one to represent you and that one will be Sam." When Tom said that, only the ones from the morning shift applauded, while we from the evening shift just kept silent until Sam went around shaking employees' hands and saying he not only represented the morning crew but all of the employees of RCI. When he said that, we congratulated him.

Tom said, "If anyone has any questions, let me know." Almost everyone raised their hands. After answering most of the questions from the employees, all seemed to be satisfied with what they heard Tom say. I couldn't ask him the questions I was going to ask because some of the employees had already asked him. We all left out with a positive mind.

Getting on the bus, David said, "Let's go to Prince George Plaza. The treat is on me." We weren't that far from it, as it was in

Hyattsville, MD. The plaza was jam packed, and man, I mean filled with people. After all, it was Saturday and a lovely day. When we went to the food areas, all the workers chose to eat at McDonald's. While we were waiting in line, everyone seemed to be happy about what they heard at the meeting. But then, a conflict broke out when some employees from another company said, "Look at them. They think they're all that because they have a union now. It's about time."

When we all looked behind us to see who was saying the words, it was another company similar to ours. We at RCI didn't hit it off well with that company: UPS. As their workers waited in line behind us to order, they continued to talk shit, saying their company was better and stretched out to other states, while RCI did not. David looked at the guy who was standing behind him saying those words.

David said to the UPS employee, "Say that shit again!" Before I knew it, all hell broke loose. David socked him right in the face. The workers from UPS came at us. The workers and I from RCI went at them. Punches were being thrown left and right. Before everyone knew it, the security guards in the mall had called the police, and they were there in no time. We were all arrested and taken to the police station in Hyattsville, MD. At the station, the police sergeant looked at me and the other RCI employees and said, "Does Matthew still work there at RCI?"

We all said, "Yes."

The sergeant said, "He and I grew up together in Jasper, TX. Matthew was a true pioneer cowboy." While we were having the conversation with the sergeant, one of the UPS workers threw up his middle finger when the others workers were getting ready to leave out. Stephen, who had just started working for RCI a month ago, exchanged words with him. It looked as though another conflict was getting ready to break out.

The police sergeant said, "Quiet all of you, or else this time, I *will* put all of you in jail. I'm going to put an end to all of this between these two companies. I will have a contest here at the police station between y'all. Batman versus Green Hornet. Oh, my bad!" When the police sergeant said that, he smiled. Then, he said, "RCI versus UPS. Whoever wins the contest, each employee will get a $500 gift card. Now y'all talk about it. UPS already said yes."

I look at Richard, James, and the others and said, "Let's do it, guys."

When I said that, they said, "Bring them on!"

The police sergeant said, "The contest will be to see who can unload five trucks in the back of the police station faster. The two trucks will be on different sides. Be here tomorrow at 10:00am." When we all said yes, we were all ready to leave the station. The employees of UPS got in front of us and said, "Wait 'til they leave; then, y'all can go." After they left, we went. All of us were talking about the contest and how we were going to kick their asses.

When we all got off the bus at Addison Station, everyone went home. At least, I think they did. I got to my castle or apartment (I had grown accustomed to calling my apartment "the castle.") When I got in, I called my mom to see how she and everyone else in Dale City, VA were doing.

"Everyone is about the same," she said. "How is the job coming along?"

"It's good, Mom," I said. "I got a savings account, and I've been saving. And, when the time is right, I'm going to move to another apartment house. How's Antoinette?"

"Antoinette is doing fine. She's at work now, Sam. But, I will let her know you called and were asking about her."

"I'm getting ready to go to bed, but I will call you tomorrow. I love you, Mom."

"I love you, son." When I hung up my phone, it never crossed my mind before that Maryland was right next to Virginia. But, talking on the phone made me feel like I was calling all the way from California.

After jumping on my bed, I dozed off. When the next day came, I got up as usual, took my shower, and then looked at the news for a little bit. Before I was getting ready to leave out, they brought up some breaking news: the FBI was still investigating companies that have contracts with the post office. I had almost forgotten about how the FBI showed up at RCI, causing almost everyone in the company to panic.

When I left out, while walking down the hallway, I heard an aggressive voice saying, "Don't forget this week we are going out for dinner. Remember that." When she said that, I started wondering if she was stalking me. I already knew she was bipolar, and when not taking her medicine, she would go into a rage.

When I got to the bus stop, I shut that thought out of my mind and started thinking about the contest we had with UPS. After getting on the bus and getting to Addison Station in no time, the employees from RCI were there saying loudly, "Let's kick their asses." It took about five buses to get us there. When we got off the bus, there were UPS busses there that their employees had ridden on. In the police station, the guys from UPS said, "We are going to make y'all look like a pile of shit." David looked like he was getting ready for a fight.

I told him, "Not now, Dawg. Let's prove we are better than they are by loading these trucks."

When we all got in line, the police sergeant said, "Are your engines ready?"

Everyone on both sides said, "Yes!"

"Then, let the show begin! 5, 4, 3, 2, 1! Go!"

Everyone took off running at high-speed. UPS was keeping up with us. I don't think I had ever run that fast in my life. When it was over, we RCI had won the contest. UPS left out angry, with bitterness in them, without saying anything.

David yelled out to them, "Y'all ain't nothing but sore losers. Talk shit now!" They looked around but didn't say anything. They just left. We at RCI found the police sergeant and thanked him for having the contest. We all got our gift cards and left out. It was just a great day for RCI. When we got to Addison Station, we all jumped on the 266 bus and, as usual, went down Central Avenue. Next, we walked down the dirt road and then went into the cafeteria. As we went in, the lights were all off, as if the company didn't pay its light bill. As we stood there, the lights came on. Gene, Peter, Cindy, and Dorothy had a big cake. On it read, "Congratulations to the employees of RCI." All of the employees looked like they were getting ready to break down in tears.

Matthew said, "Now, you workers know how much we the supervisors of the company really care about you. When y'all are finished with the cake and other good things, if y'all want to, y'all can take the rest of the day off or stay and work. Either way, you still will be paid." As anyone could guess, everyone took that day off. We all went back down to the dirt road, got on the bus, went to Addison Station, and chilled out a little. We laughed and talked about how we defeated UPS. Then, everyone said, "See you tomorrow."

When I got back home, as I crossed the street, walking to my apartment, I said to myself, "I'm going to go ahead and take Rhonda out today and get that off my shoulders." When I got to the apartments, I went and knocked on her door. When she opened it, before I could say anything, she said, "I'm ready to go out to dinner, Samuel, when you are." She had a big smile on her face, as if she knew I was going to take her out that day. Then, I took a little bird bath. When I went to go out, before I could close my door, there she was in the hallway looking, I have to say 'gorgeous.' When I told her how lovely she looked, she smiled and said, "I knew you were going to say that, Sam."

After that, we left out and went to a restaurant in Georgetown where we had a ball. She was not the same woman that I had seen at the Japanese restaurant. When we went back home, we talked a little. Then, she said, "Samuel, we must do this again," as if we were already in a relationship together.

Hearing those words, I looked her in the face, as I was about to say, "You are crazy woman!"

Then, she said, "What's wrong? You act as if you don't want this relationship to work out. THAT'S FINE. Don't say another DAMN THING to me again. It's over for good."

From that day on, she didn't say anything to me. Was it really over between me and her?

Trouble in Paradise

The next day at work, everyone was on the floor working, looking like they were pleased with how it worked out at the fire station a few days ago. Tom and Sam walked around talking with one another. Cindy came up to me and said, "You are doing excellent on the job." After that, she and I became very close. The trucks were still coming in, with more and more money being transferred than ever before. RCI's business was continuing to grow. The employees that were doing a great job were starting to get big bonuses. It just couldn't have been a better time for RCI. Employees were running out jumping in cars, speeding down that dirt road and even speeding around Addison Station, thinking we were untouchable. There were even times when I went home so worn out that I went to bed sleeping in my uniform and waking up my thinking I was in somebody else's apartment, saying, "I can't believe I didn't miss one day." On the job, everything was looking normal.

Then one day all of a sudden, Gene, Cindy, Tina, and Dorothy came running out of the office yelling, "Get out of this damn building now! We just received bomb threats!" Every one of us took off running, out of the building. When we got out, there were fire trucks everywhere. The bomb SWAT team checked all over the building. Matthew said we would meet in the cafeteria when it was over. SWAT looked all over but found nothing.

When we went back in the building, Matthew told us to sit down but said nothing after that. While we were sitting down, postal inspectors and an FBI agent came in blaming some of the employees. That's when I saw a part of Cindy I had never seen before.

She told them, "Wait one fucking minute! What gives you the right to point the finger at any of the employees of RCI? Do you have any proof that employees of this company made a threat on the company they work for?"

One of the postal inspectors said, "We are not saying that all of the employees made these threats, but the information we have from the investigation points out that one or more workers from RCI, or someone who once worked for the company, made those threats." When he said that, Cindy was getting ready to say something again. Matthew cut her off and said, while pointing his finger at the postal inspector who made the comment, acting very tenaciously, "If you have any proof, show it to me out here or either in my office."

When he said that, the postal inspector backed off and said, "I can't do that."

The FBI agent said, "This investigation will continue to go on. As for now, I have no more to say." Then, he and the postal inspectors left out. The other employees and I started clapping because Matthew had defended us. When we went back to work, Cindy came over and hugged me and smiled. That was something I will never forget. She gave me that kind of look that says, "Where have you been all my life?"

She then said, "Sam, you will continue to be the weigher of this company. But, I also have a new assignment for you. Wait here until I go in the office and get the papers I want you to sign." I couldn't figure out what the papers would say. As I was thinking, she came back with them and said, "Before you sign, read first."

I looked at them, and when I did, the papers said I had the authority to open any boxes or packages if they were suspicious. At first, I didn't want to sign the papers, but I had been with the company going on a year and had won their trust. I signed. Then, she said,

"Samuel, come in the office, Matthew and the other supervisors want a minute to talk with you." When Cindy and I walked to the office together smiling at each other, some of the employees, even the ones that I didn't get along with, gave me thumbs up. When I went into the office, Gene, Tina, and Dorothy asked the question, "Can you do it?"

I said, "Yes." From then on, I had the authority to open anything that came off the trucks. When I went back on the floor, the other workers looked at me and were quiet that night.

When everyone punched out, Tina said, "Let's go. I'm going to make a stop at the liquor store."

When we were about to head out, Cindy said, "I will take you home myself tonight," and looked at Tina with an aggressive look.

Then, Tina said, "I'll see you tomorrow."

When Tina walked off, Cindy had a strange smile on her face and said, "Let's go, Sammy boy." When we went to the car, Cindy was driving kind of slow and told me everything about her life, her ups and downs on jobs and relationships. Then, she said, "Now, tell me something about you."

I said, "Cindy, what you just said about your life matches mine, too. We both had the same kind of lifestyle." When she dropped me off, before I got out, she put her hand around my neck and kissed me.

She said, "I have known you, Samuel, for about five months, and I'm in love with you because you are innovative. You can always get the job done." When she said that, I didn't know how to respond. I just got out the car and told her I would see her the next day. I went to my apartment.

The next day, I got up, showered, and took the trash out. There was a note on my door, stating my lease was up the next month, and I had five days to sign another one or else I will lose my apartment. I called Renée and asked how things were going.

She said, "Fine. Dr. Peterson is seeing a patient now, and Yvonne is giving me news on what happened in the neighborhood yesterday."

I told her I needed to speak to Yvonne right away. Renée said, "Okay, just one minute." Yvonne came to the phone and asked me what was going on. I told her about the lease, how I had to sign it in five days or lose the apartment, and how I wanted to check out some other apartments.

She said, "I will be off on Friday, and I'll be able to take you around to see a couple of apartments, but you know you have to pay me for gas, Sam."

I said, "No problem. I will give you a little bit more."

Yvonne said, "I know you are. I will pick you up at 9:00am. Be ready or else. You know me. I will take off. You know me, Sam."

"Yes, I will be ready."

When I got off the phone, I went to the office and saw Antoinette. "How are you doing?" she said. "Are you here to sign another lease, and how is your job treating you?"

"Fine. Everything is going well, just the way I was hoping it would." As she was getting up to give me the lease to sign, I said, "Antoinette, I'm going to be moving out about the first of the month." When I said those words, I saw another side of her that I had not seen before. She went off.

"What the hell do you mean you're going to move out? What… this place ain't good enough for you? I thought you were cool, but you ain't worth two cents! Go ahead and move your damn ass out! I wouldn't miss you! Now, get the hell out of my office!"

When I left out, I was in a way kind of laughing at the way her body language went.

Time went by fast. That week when I went to work, after punching in, I went on the floor. There were a few people there. Everyone hadn't arrived yet. I went to the back. The forklift operator only had brought a couple of boxes off the truck. When they were placed on the scale, I was to take the first five boxes up to the office. But, I forgot one.

When I went back to get it and was taking it to the office, I decided to open it. When I opened it, I said to myself, "Oh, shit!" There were hundreds of Social Security checks in there. I did not believe they were supposed to be sent to RCI. I closed the box up quickly. When I took it to the office, Gene, all the supervisors, plus Sam, our representative, were there with pizza and sodas, eating and talking. When they saw me, they said, "Sam, the pizza and soda is on us."

I said, "No, thank you. I'm going back to get the rest of those boxes. I don't want to lose any time."

Then Matthew said, "Now, that's what I call a true employee of RCI." All the supervisors seemed to be impressed with me not wanting to take the time off, but Matthew looked at me in a way, I still believe to this very day, which said he knew I saw those checks in the box. The forklift operators and I were hitting it off pretty good. They started talking, saying a lot of things RCI was doing were illegal. I don't think they realized I already knew what was going on and what was in those boxes.

Tina came out and asked the people what they wanted for lunch. It was almost that time for that play of 'going out the back.' She had everybody's order and asked me what I wanted to order. I said, "Oh, let me see," with a smile on my face.

She said, "You think your ass is all that because you are on salary."

I bowed my head and said, "Yes," although she didn't say anything about it. She continued taking orders.

Once lunch break came, we all were in the cafeteria: Richard, Rita, Stephen, Gina, and the rest of the crew on the evening shift. As Tina and I were sitting down eating and drinking, we start having what seemed to be regular conversation. Then, she said something that struck a nerve. Tina looked at me right in the face and said, "Its headquarters are located in Baltimore MD, and millions upon millions of people get it every month, and some of it came here today, Sam. Do know what I'm talking about?" When she said that, her eyes were standing up. She asked me if I knew anything about it. I was silent for some time, wondering if Matthew put her up to ask those questions to see if I would answer them honestly, which I did, saying, "Yes, Tina. Social Security checks did come in one of the trucks."

The other employees in the cafeteria were a distance away, so they did not hear us discuss the matter. Tina said to me, "Listen carefully, Samuel. When you took this job, it was told to you whatever happens inside this building is not to be told to anyone who does not work for this company." After she said that, she then said something that petrified me. "I know you will be moving to another apartment this week, your lease is almost up, and you don't want to sign another one." When she said that, she smiled and said, "You know something, Sam? Those apartments in Forestville, MD fit you perfectly." When she said that, I was devastated at the things I found out about that I didn't know when I started working for RCI. The company was watching its employees when they were not at work.

After lunch was over, we all went back on the floor and things seemed normal. All of a sudden, a fight broke out between James and another employee, whom I think just started working for the company. James reached in the back of his uniform, pulled out a pistol, and held it to the guy's head, which made some employees a little nervous. Matthew and the supervisors were in a meeting in the office. Tina who was not there at the time for what reason I don't know went to James, begging him to put the gun down. She said, "What's wrong with you? Are you losing your mind?" Tina then took him outside of the building. The new employee was still there, looking anxious.

I was not too far away from them when the matter happened. I went up to the guy and said, "Things are going to be alright, man."

When we left out for the day, or should I say night, Cindy dropped me off. I said, "Thanks."

Then, as I was about to ask her if I could have the next day off, so I could see about another apartment, she said, "Yes, Samuel, take tomorrow off to see about an apartment. Don't worry. I already told Matthew you would be off tomorrow. Take care."

Laying a New Foundation

When I went inside, I started looking around, wondering if my place had been bugged. I lay down and thanked God I had made it to another day on the job.

When I got up, I called Yvonne and said, "I'm ready. I got up a little early."

She then said, "Come outside." After hanging up, I was about to go out, but when I opened my door to go out, I then backed up and shut the door a little, not locking it. I went back to my bedroom, picked up the phone, looking all around, trying to see if an intruder was in the room or on the phone. I said to myself, "I don't see anything." I turned to go out my bedroom, and Yvonne was standing there almost causing me to have a heart attack.

She said, "Boy, you act look you saw a ghost in the bedroom!"

"Oh, oh," I said.

She said, "Let's go." When we got in the car, as we went down Marlboro Pike, I was looking all around in the car, especially when we stopped at the light. Yvonne yelled out, "What the hell is your problem? You act like you just saw a UFO!"

On the way to the apartments in Forestville, Yvonne said, "Do you know the name of those apartments you want to check out?"

I said, "Yes, just one apartment complex, and that's the Doral Apartments, across the street from Forestville Mall."

Yvonne took a deep breath and said, "You mean to tell me you took a day off your job to just to look at one apartment?"

"I have already talked to the landlord, and she said to come by today and they would show me three different apartments. They are the family members that own the apartments. They don't look at one's bad credit."

"Okay Mr. Know-It-All."

When we got there and parked in front of the rental office, Yvonne said, "This place is not that bad. I have passed by here but have never come this close to it before."

When I went inside the office, the landlord Miss Brown said, "Can I help you?" She seemed very alluring.

I said, "Yes, do y'all have any apartments for rent now?" When I said that, Yvonne looked at me as if she was getting ready to interrupt.

She said, "I thought you said you already had the place…"

Before Yvonne could finish her sentence, Miss Brown said, "Yes, I think we do. Come and follow me." She smiled. I looked at Yvonne and smiled.

She said, "Boy, you are a trip!"

There were three openings in the apartment building at the 2727 Lorring Dr. complex. Miss Brown showed me the two openings on the first floor, which I didn't like because they were not immense enough. Then, Miss Brown showed me the one on the third floor, which was perfect. I liked the quadrant the apartment was in. I told Miss Brown, "I will take it." Going back to the office, I signed the lease right away and gave the first month's rent plus the deposit.

She then said, "Samuel, when would you like to move in?"

I said, "On the first of the month- tomorrow. I will synchronize things with my job and clean up the apartment that I'm at now."

She said, "That will be fine." She shook my hand and said, "Welcome to Doral Apartments. It is good to have someone living in our community who is serious about living here. Thank you again." As she spoke, I saw she was very sensual.

As I left out, I didn't know that Yvonne had left before I did and was waiting in the car. When I got there, she said, "Sam, why did you lie to me? You said you had already talked to the people about the apartment when you know you didn't. Why?"

I said, "Yvonne, I just had that strange feeling and intuition that I was going to get it. I can't describe it."

"That's bullshit!" Yvonne said. "Look, I will move you, but don't lie to me again or else you won't get another favor out of me again! Do I make myself clear?"

"Yes, ma'am," I said.

Then, she said, "When would you like to move?"

I said, "Saturday."

She responded, "Okay, you know I'm going to charge you more because of your lies, Samuel."

I said, "What?"

With a smile, she said, "Got you! Boy, I'm not going to overcharge you." When she took me back home, she said, "Be prepared tomorrow. I will be here at 9 a.m. sharp."

I said, "I will." Thanking her, I got out the car and headed to my apartment. Then, I said, "Oh, shit! I forgot I have to work tomorrow!" I turned back to see if Yvonne was still there, but she had taken off. When I got back to my apartment, I thought to myself, *I will call RCI tomorrow morning to speak with Matthew about taking tomorrow off.*

Before I hit the pillow, for some odd reason, I continued to think about Rhonda. Those thoughts wouldn't leave my mind. Did I still have feelings for her and were those feelings good? I yelled out loud to myself, "STOP! Get her out of your mind and go on with your life." I continued yelling those words, until I finally went to sleep.

The next morning, I called RCI and spoke with Sam. He told me Matthew was busy. I told him about moving into another apartment and how I had been saving my money for that since working on RCI to have a better environment to call home. Sam said, "Matthew will be back in twenty minutes. I will tell him about you moving to another apartment. I'm sure he won't mind, but call back anyway."

My response was, "Thank you." After getting off the phone, I continued packing my boxes, which I had started two days before. A few minutes went by quickly. Before I knew it, Yvonne was bumping her horn. I went out, and she had her brother and cousin, who helped me before when I moved. It looked like the same U-Haul truck, too.

It didn't take too long to get everything into the truck. As we took off down Marlboro Pike, I was a little quiet, not talking for most of the drive there. Yvonne said, "Okay, what's wrong. This is not the Samuel D. Webster that I know."

I looked at her and said, "I was just thinking about a couple of things."

She pulled the truck over and said, "I have known you for a long time. You had a serious look on your face when you said that. If something is deeply on your mind and you feel you can't deal with it, you can always come to me and talk if you want to. Let's get you to your new apartment." While we were discussing personal things, Yvonne's brother got out of the car and came over to the truck asking if things were okay. Yvonne said, "Yes, get back in the car. Let's go."

After we took off, I began feeling a little better, but those emotional feelings still continued to haunt me. Rhonda, my next door neighbor, who I took out twice and at times was uncontrollable, but for some strange reason, I missed her. When we got to the office, Miss Brown gave me the keys and said, "If anything happens, call the office right away."

"Miss Brown, once again, thank you." At my new apartment, Yvonne and I got out the truck and looked at the building. She said, "You're finally here."

"This is the place that I have been saving my money for, and I'm here."

Yvonne said, "Come on. We have to hurry up and get your stuff in there. I have some things to do." She looked around to where her brother and cousin should have been parked, but the car they were in was nowhere to be seen. As a matter of fact, her brother and cousin were nowhere at all. She threw her hands up saying, "Where the hell are they?" Before she could say anything else, they pulled up and seemed to be a little intoxicated. When Yvonne saw that, she really flew off the handle saying, "Both of y'all ain't nothing but dupes. Why did y'all have to get drunk at this time?" Then, turned to me and said, "Sam, which apartment are you in?"

I said, "Apartment 301."

Once I said that, she really got irritated saying, "I thought you said Apartment 101."

I said, "No, Yvonne. I wish I was on the first floor."

She said, "Oh, well." When her brother and cousin came over and helped to start to unload the truck, Yvonne said, "I will deal with y'all later on."

As we were taking the things off and up the steps, the people in the apartment complex did what all people do when a new person moves into the complex: stand at their buildings looking or watching from the windows. Some of them seem to be very interested, and others were a little cautious. As we took the boxes up the stairs, a lady came out of her apartment on the second floor and spoke to me saying, "How are you doing? My name is Jacqueline and yours?"

"Samuel," I said.

"Glad to meet you, Samuel. I'm on my way to work. Now, if you need anything, don't hesitate to ask me. I'll see you again." She then shook my hand and left. Meeting her for the first time, she seemed to be very interesting.

Yvonne's family members took the books up first, which were the hardest. Then, we took up the furniture. After a couple more boxes, we were finally finished. After going down the stairs, we all were worn out, even her brother and cousin. I paid Yvonne, and she said to me, "You are now in a better and more immense apartment, and you will feel a lot better."

"I already do." After going into my apartment, I looked around at books, boxes, and the furniture that I had. They were scattered all over the place. I found a spot to sit, and in one of the boxes, I took a sandwich and a bottle of water out and just sat down and ate, thinking about how I had come that far from Virginia to the projects and Capitol Heights, then to a better place in Forestville, MD. I called Renée and told her about my apartment and how long it would take me to get adjusted to it.

Renée said, "When moving to a nice place that you once thought was unachievable, when one does get it, it still seems like a dream until you see it is real. But, you will manage."

I said, "Renée, you always have the right words to say."

She laughed and said, "Sam, I will always be here for you in the time of need. That's what true friends are for."

I said, "Renée, if…"

Before I could finish my sentence, she said, "I know what you're getting ready to say.. if, I need anything to let you know." When Renée said that, I started thinking, she seemed to be intuitive, the one who has the ability to understand or know without evidence.

My response was, "How did you know I was getting ready to say that?"

She said, "Sam, you have been saying that for years."

I said, "You remember."

She said, in a humble way, "Yes, I do." Then, she said, "Samuel, I got to go, but we will talk again."

After hanging up, I just sat for some time in the same spot thinking how Renée and I were still used to one another. Then, I got up and started putting the furniture in the right place. I took a couple of boxes to the bedroom and some to the kitchen. After that, I set up my books and TV, until everything was in the right place. Then, I left out heading for Arby's to get a bite to eat.

As I walked down Lorring Drive, I saw a couple of workers from RCI, on the J-14 bus. I found out later that there was another bus to get to work. After I got in the mall, I noticed all the great stores that were in it. The best thing about it was I lived across the street.

As I walked feeling excited that I had put myself ahead in life, I was headed to the food court. When I saw all the fast food restaurants, I decided to order from McDonald's. While waiting in line, I heard a loud voice yelling and asking, "WHAT THE HELL ARE YOU DOING HERE? ARE YOU FOLLOWING ME?"

When I turned around, there she was- Rhonda! Almost all the people in the court who were in line turned around and started looking. I told the cashier I would take my order to go. When I got it, I left. Before I knew it, I heard footsteps behind me. When I looked, who else would it be but her? As I picked up speed, I went to the bookstore and stayed there for about twenty minutes. I didn't want her to know where I had moved. When I came out, I didn't see her anywhere in sight.

Proceed with Caution

I went back to my apartment and was passing through the second floor. My neighbor Jackie introduced herself once again and said, "Remember, if you need anything, let me know."

My response was, "Thank you."

When I got inside my place, I lay down and waited for the next day to come. When it did, I arose and noticed my TV was not on. I forgot that I turned it off the night before. After using the restroom, I went back to the bedroom. I was getting ready to turn it on, but something told me not to. So, I went back to sleep after a couple of hours.

I jumped up yelling, "Oh, shit!" I rushed to take a shower. After that, I took off running down the steps and across the street, to wait for the bus to show up. When it came, I got on it. I noticed the people were very quiet, as if they were deaf or speechless. I had ridden on those buses many times before to Prince George County, MD, and it had never been like that before. It was very strange.

While on the bus, I was hoping and praying that I would not lose my job. When I got there, as I went into the cafeteria, and I saw the employees from the morning and evening shifts sitting in chairs looking at TV, which was located on the left side. They looked as if they were about to break down in tears. Looking at them, I was wondering what was wrong. I turned to the TV and saw something that devastated me. I will never forget it for the rest of my life: A plane crashed into a large building, which was the Twin Towers in New York City.

As Matthew and the other supervisors were there, he said to all the workers from the morning and evening shifts: "We as employees of RCI have had our arguments and disputes with one another, but when a crisis comes along, a strong company puts its disagreements to the side. We as a nation are under attack from who we do not know as of yet. Let all of us bow our heads in silence for five minutes."

After it was over, there was a special report from CBS News about another plane crash at the Twin Towers. Then, later there was an attempted attack on the Pentagon, in Arlington, Virginia. DEVASTATED JUST DEVASTATED!

Matthew said to all the employees, "If everyone here feels they need today off, I understand."

Most of the workers, including myself, took that day off. Before leaving the building, Matthew said to me, "Sam, I would like to see you in the office now." When he said that, I felt a little irritated. Getting to the office, Matthew said, "Do you know why I called you to the office, Sam? If it wasn't for the incident happening, I would have fired the hell out of you." In the minute he said that, he was angry. He continued, "But, I will give you one damn chance. Don't fuck that up! Now, get out of my office!"

When I left, I didn't realize it at first, but the 9/11 tragedy is what saved me from being fired. When I went to the parking lot, I saw all the workers with their heads down, as if they were grieving. When I got in the car with Tina, she looked as if she had been crying all day. I took my arms and put them around her, showing my support for her and said, "Don't worry. We will get through this."

She said, "Sam, thanks. I needed that."

When we left, Tina stopped at the liquor store on Branch Avenue, across the street from Addison Station and got some vodka. When I

saw that, I was kind of astonished. When we got back in the car, Tina said, "Sam, forgive me, but I need something to relax me, especially my nerves."

Although I have never drunk and don't approve of alcohol, I still said to her, "I understand." I told her about my new apartment and that I had moved to Forestville, MD.

When we got there, she said, "This is a nice place you have. It's closer to the job than your other place." Before getting out, I asked Tina if she was going to be alright and at work the next day. She said, "Yes." I told her to take care, and I hugged her.

When I went in, I didn't know what to think. I was still wondering if it was other Americans who had made the attacks. That night, I paced back and forth in the living room in my apartment. When the morning came, the tragedy was on CNN, CBS, and ABC. The tragedy left a lot of Americans angry, who felt their country had deceived them. A news anchor reported that the United States had gotten a warning a month ago that something like that was going to happen. I listened to the news for about two hours.

Finally, I got on the phone and called my mom, asking her how she was doing. She said, "Fine. I'm okay. How are things up there?"

I said, "They are good." After a couple of minutes talking, I told my mom I would get back in contact with her later.

"Okay. Take care."

"I will, Mom. I love you." After hanging up, I called Renée to see how she was doing. As others, she was devastated by what happened and was asking questions, such as, "Why?"

I tried to console her saying, "Renée, I do believe this country will get to the bottom of this."

As I continued talking, with a flash, a news report came on saying, "This is the CBS Special Report." I told Renée I would call her later. After hanging up the phone, I saw on the news that the

United States had received a warning weeks ago. A lot of people in New York and all over the country were outraged. The report showed people yelling, "TELL US THE TRUTH!"

While I was watching, something flashed through my mind. In 1994, I was working for a company called Presearch Inc. in Fairfax, Virginia. I was a mail clerk, and as at RCI, I did a great job, always trying to perfect my performance. One day at my desk, I noticed something strange about one of the letters. My supervisor Jimmy had told me one time before that if I got suspicious about the mail, I could open it up. So, that's what I did. There was a letter from a lady named Susan. I can remember her first name but not her last. She was from Syracuse, New York and grew up in Manhattan. She graduated from Yale University and seemed to have all the advantages that any person would love to have after college. She had a good job and was married, but she couldn't deal with what she was going through. In the last sentence, she said, "I'm going to end it here right away. I will kill myself." After reading it, I took the letter to Jimmy and told him about it. He said he would take care of it. Did he? I don't know.

After listening to a little bit more news, I left out and went to get on the bus and noticed there were some police officers asking people where they were going. After the officers saw my uniform and the three letters RCI on it, they said, "Go ahead." The people on it were quiet and the police were watching everyone carefully like a hawk. Getting off the bus, I saw a vast amount of police officers in the area next to RCI, which was the post office. When I got off the bus, there were a few employees outside talking when I got there. The other workers went in going to the front. The police officers went in right away with warrants. Mary, Cindy, Tina, and the other supervisors came out, but I didn't see Gene. They said, "Go ahead and let them search, but if they ask you any questions, remember to take the Fifth Amendment."

As the police searched, they didn't find anything. They said to the supervisors, "Thanks for your cooperation." When they left out, Matthew came out of the office and said to us, "I didn't come out when the officers were searching, and some of you probably wonder why. I was talking to the Chief of Police on the phone about this. So far, we're in the clear." As things tried to return back to normal, our reputation only continued to get worse. There was even a short article in The Gazette paper about the investigation that was still going on.

That day, the 'going out the back' time came, and everyone that ordered got their lunch- all of us. At that time, all the employees seemed to have a lot on their minds, and for the first time since I started working for the company, I had never seen the employees serious like they were that day. Even James was serious. No one was angry. They were concerned about how they were going to pay their house notes, while others talked about car payments if RCI collapsed. Some said if it did, all of us would be in a big financial mess. Unemployment would not be enough to make the payments that we all had.

I stood up and said, "Even if RCI closes down here, we could ask Matthew if we could be transferred to the RCI in Detroit or Pittsburgh." When I said that, some started to bow their heads and say, "That's not a bad idea." I think some of the employees were just tired of living in Maryland and wanted to get a fresh start in another state.

As I and some others walked in the hallway and went to the floor, everyone was doing their work. Then, one of the employees came out screaming and saying, "Who the hell broke into my locker and stole my shit?" The employee was denouncing almost everyone at RCI. James went over and said to him, "Man, you are going to have to cool off."

"Get the fuck out of my business! You don't have anything to do with it! You are not a supervisor." The employee who was hollering at us, I didn't know him. Sam, the representative, and Dorothy both came out of the office and said, "What's going on out here?"

"Somebody broke into my locker and took my things!"

Sam and Dorothy said, "We will try to find out who did it. That's all we can do."

The guy said, "I had something very important in it." Then, the guy walked away, but that was not the end of the story.

When I got home that night, I turned on my TV and saw the movie *The Fish that Saved Pittsburgh*, which made me think how it would be to live and work in that city.

When I got into work the next day, the Postal Inspector was there. David told me that the Postal Inspector was checking on the building and that the post office had received bomb threats. That's why there were so many police officers around. Going into the cafeteria, Willie, Rita, James, and some of the other employees that I knew were talking about the 9/11 tragedy. I got into a conversation, which turned out to get chaotic after I gave my point of view. So many others gave theirs about it and said, "Whoever did this wicked thing, he or she should get the electric chair."

Then, I said, "Whoever did this evil I believe was from the Middle East."

When I said that, Bruce said to me, "Mr. Know-It-All, remember the attack in Oklahoma City in 1995 by Timothy McVeigh? Was he from the Middle East? Answer that question if you know so much." Although I didn't agree with Bruce and he would get out of hand once in a while, I always respected him because of his age. But, that was one time I didn't. As the argument went on, Matthew came in having the real paper that is used for printing money. The FBI wanted to talk with one of the employees from RCI. When I heard the news, I started thinking about the altercation that the employee had with some of the supervisors about someone breaking in his locker.

When I got home some of the neighbors who I didn't know were looking at me and asking me what happened. At the time, I didn't know, but if I did, I wasn't going to tell them shit. When I got inside my apartment, I turned on the TV, expecting regular news that I hear every day. Then, they brought a how there was a seizure that night at an apartment complex in Temple Hills, MD, where some people were arrested for fraud and real paper that is used by the government. My ear was itching all that day. *Something is going to happen at RCI, and I'm going to be right in the middle of it*, I thought.

Almost the whole day, I just lay back and chilled. When the next day came, before I could get up, there was some hard knocking on my door saying, "Mr. Webster, this is CBS News. Are you there?" When I got up and went to the door and opened it, the first thing they said was, "Do you work for RCI?" as they showed me their uniforms. When I said no, they asked me if I knew the employee the police arrested. "No," I said. Then, they asked how long I worked for RCI. I said very loudly, "NONE OF YOUR BUSINESS!" and shut the door in their faces.

Later, when I got to work, the Prince George County police were there arresting the guy whose locker was broken into and had the paper. The police said in an aggressive way, "We will be back." When the officers left, we knew they were going to court to get a search warrant and would be back. Everyone at RCI seemed to become a little agitated.

When they left, Matthew said out loud, "Everyone in here is going to go to their lockers, and if any of y'all have anything in it that's illegal, take it to your car and take it somewhere to get rid of it. This day, we are cleaning up. Do it now! Damn it, I mean do it!" Then, he said, "I will get one of the fork lifters to bring one of the trucks to the back. All of y'all have bags on your table. Put that shit in it and take it to the back, right away and put it in the truck. The supervisors and I will be in the office talking. Sam, put that DAMN

SCALE to the side and help some of the employees take that shit out of here!"

As me and the other employees started moving as quickly as possible, it was almost like the race of the Indianapolis 500. We didn't know how quickly the police were going to be back there. After everything was stacked in the truck, one of the fork lifters took off, taking it where I didn't know. The things that were in the bags, to this day, it still crosses my mind once in a while. What was in them? I don't know.

When I got home that night, I was some kind of glad because I didn't I have to go to work the next day. When the morning came, I didn't get up until about 11 o'clock a.m. I did a little jogging that I had been putting off lately. When I got back, I rested a little; then, I got on the bus and headed for Addison Station. When I got off the bus, it was the first time in a long time that I wanted to see a doctor, a psychologist, to talk to about my troubles. Soon, I would make plans to do just that.

I got on another bus and decided to go to Popeye's down the street from where I used to live. When I got there, Rita from the job was there eating because she had to go in early. When I sat down to eat with her, she told me some bad news I didn't want to hear. There had already been too much of it. She said one of the employees from RCI had been found dead in the woods last night. The police had not been able to identify him yet. I sat there and shook my head.

After we were finished eating, Rita said, "I'm sorry to tell you this troubling news."

****

Three hours before going to work that day, I just sat down in my living room and broke down crying hard. I had to let it out one way or the other. After doing it, I felt it was a little relief to let it out at home rather than doing it on the job. After it was over, I did feel a little better. I got myself together and prayed to God that He would give me the strength to make it through that day.

When I left, I ran across my neighbor Jacqueline on the second floor. When she saw me, her first words were, "Hi, my neighbor. How are you? How is your job treating you and the other employees?" I had been at the apartment for two weeks, and it seemed as if she was trying to find out something on me. She then said, "I know you're on your way to work. Do you mind if I join you?"

"Sure," I said, not really meaning it. As we walked down the street, I found out a little more about Jacqueline and that she seemed to be enraptured and full of ecstasy.

Before I got on the bus, I was thinking a little about the RCI employee that was found dead in the woods. When I got to work there were police officers questioning employees. Some were breaking down crying, and others were in a state of shock over the employee that was found dead. He had a criminal record and seemed to have had some disputes with some of the employees of RCI before being fired weeks ago.

When the police left, Gene, Sam, who represented us, and Dorothy told all of us, "Let this be a lesson to all of us when doing the wrong thing. This is what happened to this employee. Leo did work for a short time, but he decided to go the wrong way and look what happened to him."

Matthew went on vacation at that time. Most of the employees were quiet that day, but still got the job done. Almost everyone was looking at one another and getting suspicious and wondering if anyone from RCI had done it. Before everyone left, Sam told us that because of the anthrax everybody on the job would have to wear small masks, covering their mouth and nose until the investigation was over. Tina had to stay for a meeting, so I asked David if he could give me a ride. He lived in the apartments across from Iverson Mall, in Prince George County, MD.

He said, "Of course, but I have to stop at my place first to pick up my things. Is that okay with you?"

I said, "Yes."

On the way there, going past Silver Hill Road in Suitland, we were talking about the tragedy of the employee that once worked there but also about wearing masks at work the next day. I was saying how RCI needed the company refurbished. While we continued to talk, out of the middle of nowhere, something happened that scared the living hell out of me. A woman with bright red hair and was stark naked jumped on top of the car. David hit the brakes so hard that she fell right over and got up and zigzagged right off into the woods. That area we were going through had a lot of woods in it.

When we got to the apartments where David lived, someone in the apartment next door was playing loud music. David seemed to be very nervous for some odd reason.

He said, "I will be back in a minute." He jumped out the car and ran upstairs to the apartment like he was running for his life. Some ladies came out the apartment where the music was blasting and started talking to me saying, "We saw David in that same uniform. The same one you have on. This is the first time we saw him in it. He told us before he owned company or business, but from the way it looks to us, he doesn't have a damn business. All he was doing was just bullshitting!"

When David came out, he looked like he was almost about to die. But, he told them with that straight look on his face and those words he put together that he was a millionaire and that he still worked and just wanted to be a normal person and live in a regular neighborhood. He added a few more words to it, and I'll be damned- they believed him. He told them he would see them on Saturday and that he was going to take them out to his mansion in Montgomery County and show them around. They smiled like they had just hit the lottery. After shaking their hands and saying, "Nice to meet you," we got in the car and took off. I just looked at him.

He said, "I know what you are going to say- I need to stop lying. But, it's not easy, especially for me. I've been doing it for a long time." Then, he burst out laughing. "I'm not saying it's right."

When he dropped me off, he said, "Remember, we have to wear those masks tomorrow."

When I went in, I lay down and went right to sleep. The next day, I did my usual thing. As I did every morning, I got up pretty early. While looking at a little TV and hearing about the big news of the anthrax attack, I decided to go to Arlington, VA and visit the Westover Apartments where I once lived. As I went up to the bus stop and was waiting, I started thinking about trying to better my life and get another job. That was the first time that had crossed my mind since working for RCI. When I got on the bus, I was quiet, just thinking about what the future was going to bring.

When I got to Addison Station, I got on the subway right away. I was kind of glad to get out of Maryland for a little while. As the subway moved into Washington, DC, the downtown area, I had a good view of the capital and thought, *This little city's population was small and doesn't have over 700,000 people, but it is considered by many as the most powerful city in the world.*

As the subway went by Foggy Bottom Station when going into Arlington, VA, there were so many metro police officers all over it. In the subway, people were looking and seemed to be somewhat enigmatic. Once going into Pentagon Station, I looked out at the side of the window and saw the damage at the Pentagon. The news reporters were all over. The Marines, Army, Navy and Air Force were there to give their respect to the ones who were killed at the Pentagon.

When the subway arrived to Ballston Station, I got out there and got on the escalator. When I got off, I looked around and saw that everything there was about the same as when I left in the year 1999. The stores that people worked at were still there, along with the banks and the senior citizens' home that I used to walk by on my way to Ballston Mall, where I used to go and hang out sometimes.

As I went into the mall, they had added new stores. After looking around, I went back to Ballston Station and waited there for the B2 bus to come. It didn't take long to come. When I got on it, I was a little anxious while riding the bus down Washington Boulevard. When the bus got to N and 16th Street, I got off. I walked up the street, and my legs began to shake a little. When I got to the front of 5805 Apartment 2, I just stood there looking as if I were in a trance or having a small seizure. While I stood and looked, some people across the street came over and said, "Are you okay?" with a smile on their faces.

I said, "Yes, I used to live here before moving to Maryland. I came to visit the apartment to see what they look like now. They still look the same." I was talking to two guys and one woman. They asked me what apartment I used to live in. I said, "Apartment 2."

"That's the one I live in," the lady said with a big smile on her face. "Would you like for me to give you a tour through it?"

I said, "Oh, yes. Would you?"

She said, "Of course." When she, the two guys, and I went in the door, my heart was really beating. I looked around the apartment and felt like I was in a time machine. I stood there in the living room just staring at the walls. It all seemed like yesterday. After what seemed to me like a few seconds turned out to be twenty minutes. When I came to myself, the people who lived across the street, who knew me from the past, said they were getting ready to call the ambulance. The lady said, "You were out for about 20 or 25, like you were daydreaming."

My response was, "Sometimes that does happen." She then showed me the kitchen and backyard. The grass was still green. After that, we went up the stairs and went into the bedroom. As I looked, I saw just how nice the lady kept it. Going down the hallway, it still had that fresh smell in it. After we went down the steps, I shook the lady and two guys' hands and thanked them for showing me around the apartment. The lady told me, "You take care, Samuel. Anytime you want to come here again, you're always welcome."

I said, "I appreciate that very much. Take care." When I left, I took a deep breath and got on the bus. When I got to the subway, I jumped on and took off going through Washington and back to Maryland to Addison Station. When I got off, some of the employees were there talking about the masks that we had to wear because of the anthrax attack. When all of us got on the bus, some were talking about the anthrax and others were talking about things that didn't make sense to me. But, I was thinking about another job and possibly about going to college one day.

When we got to work on the floor, Matthew had the employees in line to get a mask. But before getting it, we had to sign our signatures first. Why? I don't know. When everyone got his/her mask, Matthew said before we put them on, "I know it's going to be hard wearing these and breathing in them, but we got orders from Homeland Security that we as well as the workers at the post office have to wear them temporarily. When we all put those masks on, oh Lord, it was unbearable, but we dealt with it.

Matthew said to me, "Go to the back before you do anything else. We just had some orders that came in." When I got to the back, there were trucks from California and Arkansas, with a huge amount of boxes. Some had those marks on them. As I took as many as I could to the office, there seemed to be more coming in. Dorothy and Tina, who most of the time didn't get along, were hitting it off, laughing and talking. Matthew brought a bottle of champagne out with him, laughing and talking with other supervisors.

As I set the boxes on one another, some of the boxes were being opened and I looked. At no time in my life had I ever seen that much money in person. All the boxes that I brought in totaled at least twenty. Matthew told me to take eighteen of them into his office. I saw him giving Tina, Mary, Cindy, and other supervisors, including Sam, the representative, hundreds of dollars. He looked at me and said, "Remember, you know nothing and saw nothing. We have to keep all things private from the rest of the world. He gave me a big bonus, which came with my next check.

I was wondering when I left out what was in the rest of those boxes that I took in the office. When I came out, some of the employees were giving me that look as usual. I returned to the back to the truck and took more boxes to the offices more times than I ever had since working there. Willie, the elderly employee, who I had words with during the time in the cafeteria, put his head up to my ear and said, "I know what's going on. I have been with this company almost longer than anyone else. I do believe I know what's going on, and there's a lot of racketeering going on with this company, and you are going to be a part of the ones who are going to get in big trouble. Remember, I warned you."

When he said that, I left out wondering and saying to myself, "He could very well know," as I started weighing some of the employees' bags. When I went up to Gina's post, she said, "Come here for a couple of minutes, Sam." When I went over, she said, "This is one of the bags that is supposed to go in the office." At first, I thought she didn't know what she was saying, until she pointed to the mark and said, "It's code." Then, she said she used to work at the post office years ago. When she said that, I just eyed her. She knew what RCI was doing just like Bruce did, and I was thinking what if she decided to go to the police and tell them everything. While I was just standing there and thinking, she said with a big smile on her face, "Sam, are you going to take my pallet out and bring me another one?" Somewhere along the way, she had become aware of the activities within the company.

I said, "Okay." When I brought her another one, she said, "Don't worry. Your secret is safe with me." After taking other employees' pallets to the back and taking them more to work on, I still was a little bit nervous about what Gina had said. I was thinking to myself, *What if she did go to the police and tell them was going on at RCI? All hell would break loose!*

On the way home, Tina said, "Sam, you seem a little tense and whatever you got on your mind, it's serious."

I whispered to myself, "You can say that again."

Then, Tina said, "What did you say?"

I said, "Nothing."

"Yes, you did. You said, 'You can say that again'," she said. Then, she said, "Sam, whatever it is, if you want to talk, I will always be here. Don't let it eat you up inside."

When I got home, I said, "Thank you, Tina, for your advice."

As I went up the stairs, Jacqueline and what sounded like her sister were arguing with one another saying, "I don't know how Mom put up with you so long!"

When I put my foot up to go to the third step, Jacqueline opened the door and pushed her sister out. As I was looking, she yelled, "Don't get involved in this!" I had no intention of doing so. When I got in my place, I called it a day.

When the next day came, my mind was on what Gina had said. I had almost forgotten all about it. I decided to go to Arby's across from the mall before going to work. I have always loved eating at Arby's since the days my father was living. I remember the Arby's on Marlboro Pike across from Benning Road, in Prince George County,

MD. My mom, sister, dad, and I used to go there back in the seventies.

When I went across the street and got up close to Arby's, I noticed that the architecture of the building of Arby's was different from the way it used to be. When I went in and made my order, I decided to eat there. While I was doing that, my mind once again was on trying to get another job. While sitting there thinking deeply, I decided to see if I could take another day off, telling them I had to go see the doctor because I was not feeling well, which physically I wasn't.

After eating, I left out heading home. I called Renée and talked with her, seeing how she, Yvonne and Dr. Peterson were doing. "Everyone is fine," she said. "How is your job coming along? Is everything still the same?"

I said, "I have been thinking about filling out applications for another job. I want to take tomorrow off and look."

Renée said, "How are you going to do that? Y'all only have three days to take all during the year."

I said, "I know. I'm going to stop by there and see you. Ask Dr. Pearson if I can see him tomorrow."

Renée laughed saying, "Anytime you want to come over here, you can. I would like to ask you a question, Sam. Do you think one day we will ever get..."

Before she could get the last word out, she was called to a meeting. She told me, "Sam, I have to go. We'll talk tomorrow." After we were finished talking, I went to the bus stop. When the bus came, I did as I always do when I get on the bus- think. I was wondering if Matthew would let me off the next day.

At work, all the employees from both the morning and evening shifts were there. Gene, Sam, Mary, Cindy, and some of the supervisors from the morning shift whose names I have not mentioned. I was familiar with one of them- Philip. He was congratulating workers for not taking any days off. When Philip awarded his employees, there were fifteen of the employees who had worked straight through that whole year. The morning shift had a high amount of workers who didn't take a day off for a year.

Cindy then named the ones from the evening shift: James, Rita, and three others, whom I didn't know. But, before it was over, Cindy said, "Oh, wait just a minute. There's another employee who I almost forgot about, Samuel." When she said that, I knew our relationship was strong. I have to confess. I did take two days off during that year. When I went up to receive the award, I thanked Cindy very much for strongly believing in me and hugged her. When everyone left and went back to the floor, I knew I had to do something I really didn't want to, but I chose to do it because I wanted to better myself and that was telling my boss a lie that I had an appointment the next day to see my doctor. So, I had to ask if I could get the next day off. When I started walking to the office, I started thinking, *Should I do this?*

When I got to the door, I was getting ready to turn back. Matthew came out and said, "What's up?" When he said that, I started mumbling. He said, "Get to the point."

I said, "Gene, I haven't been feeling too well lately and have not seen my doctor in a long time, but now I have to see him. It's a physical and mental condition. I'm really not feeling too well. And, I…"

Matthew said, "Stop. Tomorrow, go see your doctor and remember to bring back a note that you saw him." After that, he said no more. He just walked away. When I left, I got on the first bus that showed up. It was filled, as the people were getting off work. As the bus continued down Central Ave, some of the riders talked, while others, like me, were just lying back resting and waiting to get home. After arriving at Addison Station, people were rushing off. Some headed to the subway, while others to another bus.

As I walked down to where the sign J12 was located, a guy who I did not know from the apartment complex I lived at or from anywhere came up to me and congratulated me for doing a great job at RCI. Then, he said something that caused me to feel uneasy. "Good luck! You're definitely going to need it."

I looked at him in a strange way and said, "What do you mean by that?" He just walked away, and I never saw him again. When I got home, after checking my mailbox, I was headed upstairs. I saw Jacqueline, who had just opened her door. She said, "Hi, sweetie." When I looked at her, she had lingerie on and was doing.. well, it looked like to me, she was dancing, or she could have been intoxicated. When I got inside, I lay down immediately and went to sleep.

After getting up, I headed for Addison Station. When I got there, I noticed some people with RCI uniforms, but I didn't recognize those employees. They were waiting for the 266 bus and talking with one another. One of them said, "Did you get that paper out of the locker?"

The person he was talking said, "Oh, yes. We can start working on it tonight." When he said that, it was in my mind most of the day, as I tried to grasp it. I was wondering, *What are they talking about? Drugs or was it something bigger than that?*

When I got into Washington, DC, to DC Hospital, I went to the EEG lab, where it was always called the headquarters of Dr. Peterson, Renée, and Yvonne's work. When I got there, Renée was glad to see me as she always was, but she was busy and said, "Samuel, go on my computer and play a game until I'm finished." That's what I always did when going to see Renée if she was with patients. While playing a couple of games and then checking out the jobs on the computer to see what was available, I was still trying to figure out what those employees of RCI at the station were referring to. Meanwhile, I came up with a few jobs that I was interested in and that paid well. But, the locations were just too far, like Utah and Wyoming where there are few minorities. When Renée came back, she said, "Did anything come up?"

"Yeah, but they are too far."

"There are some openings for maintenance positions, but I know you aren't interested. I'm going to ask my sister to keep her eyes open."

When Yvonne came in, she said, "How are you doing, Sammy?" with a smile on her face.

"Yvonne, you are always going to be Yvonne."

"I thank you, Sam," she said back.

Then, Dr. Peterson came in saying, "How is everyone in here doing, especially you, Samuel?"

I said, "Good."

"Are you still on the job," he asked.

I said, "Yes."

Then, Dr. Petersen said something that surprised me. "I have heard a lot about RCI, Samuel. Is it really true?"

My answer was, "I take the Fifth Amendment, Doctor."

Then, he said, "Come to my office."

When I went in, he said, "What's going on?"

"There's a lot of things happening, Dr. Peterson. I see you have found it out."

"I was only joking with you when I said that."

"Believe me. There are many things that are happening at RCI, and it is taking some effect on me physically and mentally, Dr. Peterson. I have been looking for other jobs, but so far I have not come across any jobs that I'm interested in that are located in this area. Dr. Peterson, I feel like I'm almost a little on the edge although I'm not."

"I remember your father and how he did a lot for you, your mom, and your sister. Your father always tried to teach you the right things in life. Samuel, your father was a great father and friend to many who knew him. He once said, 'When you are going through hard times, always remember that there is someone out there worse than you are.' Don't ever forget that."

"I'll try to remember."

Then, Dr. Petersen said, "I have to see another patient now, Samuel, but you will get through this. I know you and believe in you."

When I left out the office, Renée asked, "How was the conversation?"

"It was good."

Renée said, "Never give up." Then, she said what she always says. "Something will come through. It always does." Then, I was about to ask her if she would like to go to lunch, but before I could ask her, she said, "I have ten patients to work on today, but when I have some time off, maybe we can go out to lunch or dinner, if that's okay with you, Sam."

"Of course," I said. She gave me that beautiful smile and said, "Bye."

When I left out, I was kind of feeling a little better. When I walked to the subway and waited for the train, I started thinking of what my parents once said, "If something is deeply on your mind, and you feel that you can't deal with it, it's always good to talk with someone, not anyone, but someone you know real well that has been with you for years that you can trust."

When I got off at Addison Station, as I was walking to catch the bus home, there was some breaking news spreading like fire all over Prince George County. Police had arrested some people last night for fraud and having heard the news, many of the employees at RCI were saying that it was one of their workers.

****

One of the new supervisors who I had never seen before told us to shut the hell up and get out the cafeteria and do our job. When he came on the floor just as I was about to get the scale, Tina came up to me and thanked me for showing consideration. I felt a little down that day. It was more than about the 9/11. It was about private things as well. I hugged her and said, "That's what friends are for." After that, I headed down to the back and did my job, but there were no secret boxes coming in that day that I had to take the office, just regular boxes and the 'out to the back' lunch deal.

As we ate lunch and talked, everyone still had their opinion about the tragedy, but the arguments slowed down a little bit but were still on the big topics of the news. As the days went on, healing started coming slowly. But then, another tragedy struck: the anthrax attack on September 18, where 18 people were killed and 17 were infected. Others, as well as myself, felt we were going through another 9/11.

When everyone was at work the next day, the employees worked and talked a little. Then, we got the news. As they broadcasted it on the news, so many people were living in fear and nobody had an answer.

Later, I went over to the Forestville Mall to Footlocker to buy a pair of Nike Air. When I left out, I went across the street to the other side, where the J. C. Penney was. As I was walking in that direction, I saw a gun store and a large amount of people who seemed to be acting out over the 9/11 happening and now the anthrax attack. Many were there to buy guns and were saying if our country can't protect us, "We will do it ourselves."

When I got home that night, as I got ready to go to bed, my apartment phone rang. Most of the time, I don't use my house phone, but just as other people, I use my cell phone. When I answered it, a very odd voice I didn't recognize said, "Tomorrow will be a special day for all the employees." After hanging up, I sat on the side of my bed, trying to figure out who it was on the phone. I still to this day don't know who it was. I thought maybe we were going have another surprise party for the employees for doing a great job. I slept well that night.

The next morning, I got up and decided to do some jogging around the apartment, which I hadn't done for a while. After I went back into my place, I ate some cereal. Then, I got on the bus. When I got to RCI, the employees started off talking a little. Then, everyone started laughing as we all were enjoying ourselves. Out of the middle of nowhere, the police officers and even the postal inspectors all came running right through the building. Before getting inside on the floor where we work, I heard a lot of shoes running through the cafeteria. When they all got on the floor, they yelled, "THIS IS THE POLICE! EVERYONE'S HANDS UP NOW! THIS IS A BUST!"

Someone inside said, "Oh, shit!" The police held everyone there in the building. Some were in handcuffs, saying they would not say anything until they saw their lawyer. Some who were arrested were in a state of shock. Unfortunately, I knew that one day that was going to happen, but not like that with the police not wanting to question none of the employees who were not arrested, which one of them was me. I just left out, walking on the opposite side of the dirt road and caught the J14 bus back home. I got there and went up the stairs. Before getting to my apartment, I said to myself, "This is the end," before going in. I looked down and saw a Washington Post newspaper. When I picked it up, I'll look through it in the employment section for mail clerk positions.

As I was looking, I fell asleep and dreamed of a company that was hiring someone who had experience with mail. I saw the company's address and decided to go there to fill out the application. When I got there, I noticed how strange the building was and how odd it looked. I had never in my life seen anything like that before. When I went in, the machines that the company had and the uniforms that the employees had on looked like something in the twenty-fifth century.

When the boss of the company came to me, he said, "Can I help you, sir?"

I said, "Yes, are you hiring?"

He said, "We are."

When I asked him the name of the company, he said something that I couldn't pronounce. When I woke up, I was in a deep sweat and shaking all over. Then, I said to myself, "That company in the dream, was it RCI?"

About the Author

Samuel D. Webster lived in DC, MD, and VA in the 90s. While living in Arlington, VA, he got started in politics, by writing letters to Congress and to senators. His writings continued on to the Clinton Administration and the Obama Administration, as he wrote letters to the White House. From all of writings, he received a response.

In 2010, he moved to L.A., where he attended L.A. Trade Tech and Los Angeles City College. At both colleges, he studied political science and journalism. He still lives in L.A. and plans to continue his goal of writing.